IN SPITE OF THE DARK

A COLLECTION OF POETRY AND PROSE

 Willow Park Press

In Spite of the Dark
A Collection of Poetry and Prose
Copyright © 2021 LUW Press

Print ISBN: 978-1-7332908-1-4

Cover design by E.B. Wheeler
Copyright Willow Park Press
Image courtesy of Tithi Luadthong via Shutterstock

❀ Created with Vellum

In Spite of the Dark is dedicated to all the creative people associated with the Brigham City Writers chapter of the League of Utah Writers. And also to the loved ones who support them.

CONTENTS

FOREWORD

In Spite of the Dark is the second anthology produced by Brigham City Writers, a northern chapter of The League of Utah Writers. A sincere thank you to all the authors and editors who made this collection a reality. Thank you to Felicia Rose for poetry editing, to McKel Jensen and Keri Montgomery for prose editing, and to E.B. Wheeler for cover and interior design.

Many of the stories and poetry included were created in 2020 at a time when the world was facing severe challenges and we longed for reassurance. The theme of this collection is that even in dark places, there can be hope. There is life in spite of loss. There is creativity in spite of pain. There is light in spite of the dark.

This collection features both light and dark themed stories and poems. The anthology committee offers this collection to you with best wishes for brighter days ahead.

LIGHT

"A little bit of light dispels a lot of darkness."
-Rabbi Schneur Zalman

1

THE ELEVATOR

KERI MONTGOMERY

Marcus stood on the hallway tile and waited as the elevator came for him. Four times in the last fifteen minutes, the sharp bell had announced the box's arrival, and four times he'd peered inside at the numerous occupants and decided not to enter. Four times the doors rattled closed and the elevator let out a slight groan as it moved, as if mocking him.

Marcus pushed the *down* button again.

A couple minutes went by, then the doors opened. This time, the elevator was empty. Marcus took a deep breath and shuffled into the void, panting a little as the doors closed.

Just as the two sides were about to touch, a hand pushed through the crack. A woman hurried in beside him.

Marcus shut his eyes. He contemplated stepping out, but the doors closed too quickly, and the elevator groaned. It was too late. The box had a mind of its own.

The woman smelled of hairspray, and she shifted her weight from one high heel to the other, all the while staring at the door instead of meeting his gaze. That was fine. Ideal, in fact. Marcus didn't make eye contact in the elevator. No one did. As if their lives were too complicated and their minds too preoccupied to acknowledge the brief meeting. After all, they lived the same moment, breathed the same air, in the same box, for only minutes of the day. There was barely room for pleasantries, let alone in-depth conversation.

He'd ridden with the woman seven times since moving into the apartment building last year. Though he still didn't remember her name, only that she was older than him by at least a decade and she owned a hand-held yappy dog that often accompanied her. The furry thing usually sniffed his elbow while the woman pretended Marcus didn't exist. Today, she didn't have the dog, and he didn't mind the absence. Instead, she carried a microwave-sized postal box marked *fragile* on the outside lid. Clearly, she was on her way to the postal drop-off pile in the lobby.

The elevator descended to the eighth floor and stopped short. A couple entered in mid-conversation—newlyweds based on Marcus's previous observations.

"Jackson, it's no big deal," the young woman said, brushing up next to Marcus as she stepped inside. She smelled of fruity perfume, but thank heaven a subtle one. "She's only my mother. Dinner won't kill you."

All of them shifted in unison—a personal space dance within the box.

The young man side-glanced at both Marcus and the hairspray lady before facing the door. "We'll talk about it later."

"When?" she asked. "When my parents are getting off a plane from Montana and you're cowering in the car?"

Jackson hard-pressed the lobby button. "Come on, Ellie. Later."

As the door closed, the atmosphere in the elevator vacuumed thin, and Marcus felt a swell of nerves percolating in the back of his head. Apparently, the honeymoon was over.

They rode down another floor, all the while Marcus trained

his gaze on the elevator's digital display screen, hands in his pockets, muscles more tight than relaxed. He was still glad the dog wasn't there to make the ride worse.

On the fifth floor, the elevator thumped to a stop. The hairspray lady steadied on her heels and brushed her manicured hand against the side-wall for support.

When the door opened, two gray-haired gentlemen, dressed in suits and pulling luggage, wheeled inside, their faces jovial with laughter.

Marcus braced himself for the noise.

"That's when I pulled off his toupee," the taller man said.

"Ha, Jerry! You didn't. I don't believe that for a second." The shorter man squeezed in next to the newlyweds. "Didn't hear screaming from the church while I was outside avoiding the widow. So, I don't believe you."

"Seriously, George. No joke. The rug came off. Best shock of a lifetime."

"End of a lifetime. The poor man was in his casket. But that explains why everyone came out clutching each other in shock. Why didn't the funeral director toss you out?" George reached over and pressed the already-lit lobby button.

"He couldn't. You know me, George. Too quick. They didn't know who did it. Hair one second, gone the next." Jerry chuckled until he snorted.

"Ah, nice sleight of hand, Jerry. I'll admit, you've got skills."

The door closed.

"Thanks for finally acknowledging it, my friend," Jerry said. "I figured the vanishing act was justified. Frank's wife liked him in that mop, but not him. He hated the toupee. Always said bald was better. So . . . at the end of his life's journey, I did what any good friend would do. I set him free."

"Frank would've been proud."

The men paused, both staring at the upper door while nodding and grinning to themselves, each lost in thought.

The elevator jerked. Marcus's mind shifted from the visual of toupee thievery at a funeral to how close the strangers surrounded him. And now there were two sets of luggage to contend with. He sucked in a deep waft of hairspray odor, and recalled his psychiatrist's instructions for tight spaces and crowds—deep breathing, relaxing the muscles, envisioning his destination instead of his current location. Just being out of his apartment was a victory, one that he'd almost mastered on a regular basis. But taking the stairs was easier. So, for the last while, the elevator had been his homework—his next step toward coping and functioning with his anxiety.

The door opened on the third floor, a bell chime ringing in Marcus's ears. He inhaled a fresh swell of precious air, stealing a chance to steady his nerves before a new passenger squeezed inside. He wasn't sure if his anxiety could endure another one.

"That's odd," Jerry said.

The six of them stared at an empty hallway.

George leaned out. "Must be those new-fangled technosensor-whatcha-doohickies. They must not be working right."

"Do you have any idea what you're talking about, know-it-all?" Jerry pulled him back inside. "Push the button again."

"Like you know anything." George bumped the lobby light and slid his knuckle across the *close door* button. "You steal toupees off dead guys."

"And I'm good at it." Jerry smiled at Jackson and Ellie, giving them a wink.

They leaned away.

When the door closed, a subtle buzzing vibrated under Marcus's feet. His heartbeat jittered with the motion, and he studied the reflective display screen while willing the number to descend from three to one. He wished for telekinesis, squinting his eyes, but the elevator remained fixed in place.

They waited in silence for about thirty seconds, nothing

changing. There wasn't motion at all, not a pull of gravity, or a settling of brakes or shifting of cables, and thank heavens not a plummeting to sudden death. The elevator was simply still. Silent. Dead. With the door closed.

"Hang on," Jackson pressed the *open door* button without success. "That's weird."

"Are we stuck?" Ellie asked.

"Maybe."

"Oh, no," the hairspray woman whispered. She clutched the postal package tight against her chest. "Why didn't I take the stairs?"

"Apparently, we all should have taken the stairs," Jerry said. "Anyone got poker cards and a stack of cash that's itching to change owners?"

Marcus tucked his hands inside his jacket pockets, but he fisted them so tight that pain shot through his palms. He counted the floor tiles, calculating the elevator's square footage.

"Everyone, wait a minute." Jackson took out his cell phone and fiddled with the screen.

Ellie did the same with her own phone. "I've only got one bar in here. Maybe I can send a text. Who should we message?"

"The super," George said. "I think this building has a super, but not sure because we're just visitors. We stayed with an old college friend while we went to the funeral. Travel costs, you know, they get expensive at the last minute. Better to book way ahead."

"No one plans their death by natural causes," Jerry said, raising an eyebrow and shaking his head. "You think Frank should have given you notification before his heart attack so you could book a hotel at a good rate? You even had a cheaper and shorter flight than me. When I get to be one hundred and one, I'll call you before I keel over in my applesauce. Will that make you happy, King George?"

"I'm just stating facts." George squared to face him. "And you won't need to call me. I'll probably be cursed to land in the same nursing home. I'll feel the applesauce splat from across the bingo table." He turned back to Jackson. "Let's message the super."

Jackson nodded. "Right. Does anyone have his number?"

They stared at each other, except for Marcus, who lowered his head until his chin nearly rested on his front collar. His mind spun, unable to remember the super's name let alone the phone number. He hoped, as he always did in his low moments, that the others couldn't decipher his body language, and he'd be invisible to deal with the anxiety on his own. It was a private battle, to remain level-headed and conquer the jitters devouring his insides. Marcus blank-stared at the lines in the floor, failing to tame his rapid breathing.

"Okay," Jackson said, glancing up from his phone. "Is this the kind of thing you call 911 for? It doesn't seem like an emergency.

"It will be if we run out of oxygen, young man," George said, thumping his hand against the metal door as if the pounding would jar it loose.

Seven tiles, eight tiles, corner tile with a chip . . . Marcus breathed in more hairspray aroma. As a distraction, he glanced at the package the woman held, reading the label. The address was to a Suzette in his building. *Suzette.* That was her name. It sounded right. But odd that she was mailing a fragile package to herself.

"I'm not getting a response to my texts," Jackson said.

Ellie groaned at her phone, flopping her arm down to her side. "Neither am I. Are we sure this thing is really stuck?" Both she and Jackson began fiddling with the button panel and digital display screen, running their fingers along the sides as if searching for a way into the system. "I don't think the emergency button is working. Maybe this is a computer glitch, not a mechanical problem," she said.

"A glitch in an elevator?" Jerry leaned on his luggage handle. "In my day, when they had a problem, you just dropped."

"Oh, yah," George said, a smirk on his face. "In your day, huh? Which is also my day. Jerry, when was the last time you dropped in an elevator? That's right, never. So watch it, Doomsday, or you'll have these young people fainting from fright."

Jerry chuckled with an accompanying snort and jabbed Jackson in the shoulder. "No, young people are tougher than they look. If anyone can hack the elevator, these two can."

Marcus scooted against the wall, gripping his sore palms on the waist-high handrail behind his back. He gazed up at the ceiling LED lights, wishing there was an escape hatch like in all the movies, and attempted to ignore that George had just planted the term "fainting" in his head. Passing out, in this tight of a space, wouldn't end well. He needed to keep the panic attack at bay.

"There's nothing to hack here," Jackson said. "Plus, sorry, I'm not a hacker. I'm about to graduate dental school. So unless the elevator needs a crown . . . " he said and shrugged.

"What about you?" Jerry turned to Ellie. "Can you figure this thing out?"

"I figure out skeletons that have been buried underground for fifty years. I'm getting my PhD in forensic anthropology. I like mysteries, but not mechanical ones. Elevators should just work."

The hairspray lady, Suzette, stepped from the corner and cleared her throat. "Look, can everyone give me a little more space. I need to sit down, and I don't want to drop this box."

They shifted, but couldn't adjust by much. Marcus wasn't able to move, no matter how fixed and determined the pleading in Suzette's expression. His feet felt like lead, tied down with chains, despite the swaying, pseudo feeling of waves attacking his mind.

"What's in the box?" Jerry asked. He leaned across Marcus to get a better view of the top label. "Sending priceless figurines to an auction house?"

Marcus winced at the closeness.

"Priceless, yes," she said. "Figurines, no." Suzette slid her back down the wall, balancing the box upright, until she sat in an awkward pretzel-ish configuration on the tile floor. "Thank you. It was getting heavy."

"Why not just set it down?" Jackson asked.

"That wouldn't be respectful."

Jerry leaned back. "So . . . what's the treasure? Anything edible?"

She grimaced, lowering her forehead toward the postal box until wisps of her black hair dusted the top label. "Certainly not." With that, she tightened her lips.

"Sorry, ma'am. Not my business, I guess," Jerry said. "Just wondering if there's anything useful for our situation inside that package. We all should pitch in, you know. For survival."

Suzette tilted to meet his gaze, her eyes glossy with tears. "It's my dog. He passed away this morning. I'm just using the box to take him to the vet for cremation. I sprayed hairspray inside to make the cardboard smell sweeter . . . not so harsh."

They quieted, leaving a silent void that filled Marcus's head with so much pressure, he thought his eardrums would implode. He tunnel-visioned on the box—the petite coffin, inside a larger coffin, filled with six people who couldn't get out and one who had to force himself to breathe. And the air wreaked of hairspray to mask a dead dog smell.

"Um, sorry for your . . . uh . . . loss," George said.

Jackson and Ellie nodded in agreement. Jerry shrugged.

George unzipped the front pocket of his suitcase. "I do have one protein bar. If we can figure out how to split the thing into six portions, it might stretch our survival to dinner time. Depending on what you all had for breakfast, of course."

Jerry shook his head. "One protein bar? That's it? That's how you prepare for a disaster, George?"

"Well, I didn't expect the apocalypse to happen on my way to the airport, did I?"

"I guess we're going to have to drink our own pee to survive," Jerry said. "Although, I suppose, if we get desperate, we can eat the dog."

"No!" Suzette clutched the box.

"But he's already dead!"

"Wait," George said. "Is it bad luck to mention death so many times in a stuck elevator? That must be bad luck somehow. We need to get out before we jinx ourselves. So . . . let's all jump at once. Maybe the thing will move or the doors will open."

"You're crazier than I am," Jerry said.

"Jumping's not a real thing in this situation," Ellie said, pointing at the tile. "If the elevator is truly stuck, there's brakes keeping it in place. We're still on the third floor, in theory."

Jerry tightened his face. "I thought you said you didn't know mechanical stuff?"

"That's just common sense. Just like a person shouldn't make an insensitive joke to a woman about her dead dog."

"Child!" Jerry straightened up. "Life without humor is not life at all. That includes death."

"Humor about death?" Ellie squinted at him. "How awful. I'm pretty sure that's not a thing either."

"Well, you're going into death as a profession. You might want to invest in a few corny knock-knock jokes to keep yourself sane."

"Now, hang on," Jackson stepped between them. "Ellie is fine just the way she is. She doesn't have to be funny."

"I can be funny!" she said.

"That's not what I meant—"

"Relax, son," Jerry said. "*You* definitely need a sense of humor. You're going into teeth."

"That's enough." Jackson held up his hands. "Ellie and I are being civil in a crisis. You should be too. Let's not get all Lord of the Flies here."

"I'm always a pillar of civility," Jerry said. "Now the real question is, which one of us will be appointed leader of our little band of survivors?"

"Me," George said, holding up the protein bar. "I'm the one controlling the food supply."

"Ugh!" Ellie rubbed her forehead. "Jackson just text 911."

"But this isn't an emergency."

George motioned wild with his hands. "It might be! How much oxygen do you think we have left? Everyone, breathe through your nose, not through your mouth."

Marcus slid down against the wall, flopping next to Suzette and the hairspray coffin. He covered his ears with his hands and stared at his knees. The others wouldn't stop. And the elevator wouldn't go. His heart raced, his head swimming with each labored muscle movement and weighted eyelid blink. It was coming—either a panic attack or complete unconsciousness. He'd never passed out in an elevator before. This would be the first time. Maybe he'd wake up in a hospital room with merciful open-air and no one talking to him. Or . . . maybe he'd not wake up at all.

"Are you alright?" Suzette whispered. She stared at him, her own eyes looking heavy as she gently cradled the postal box.

His mind spun, but he managed to nod. The response wasn't true, but it was easier.

"Me, too," she said. "I guess."

He focused on her face, specifically on the rogue tear escaping down her cheek.

"You want to know something?" she said. "My dog's name was Precious. Silly, I know. But the animal shelter named him. I couldn't think of anything better, so I left it. I had Precious for ten years. He made life easier. Better. It's not right that he's stuck in a box. Forever."

Marcus stared at the *fragile* label on the lid, and then at Suzette's weighted eyes and the red splotches forming along her freckles. For a moment, he understood what it was like to be her —fragile, but trying to be strong. He reached out his hand and gently patted her arm, sharing all he could give in the moment. Then he pulled back.

"Thanks," she said.

Ellie smacked the elevator door with her palm. "I can't be in here one more second, Jackson!"

"And *that's* how I feel during dinner with your parents!" Jackson said. "You want to have open communication in our relationship. Well, here's some brutal honesty. I'll never be good enough for your mother. I'm pretty sure she hates me."

"That's nuts. She doesn't hate you."

"Then why doesn't she ever say anything kind? Only what needs to be improved. The rest of the time, she's quiet. It's eerie."

Ellie's face flushed. "Not all of us can express what we're feeling at the exact moment we feel it. That's too hard sometimes. My mother can't always find the right words, but she does have emotions, Jackson. She's proud of you. She told me so at Christmas."

Jackson stared at her for a moment, then slumped against the railing like a stubborn child, his head down and his arms folded tight against his chest. His whole body seemed to slouch as he exhaled a deep sigh.

"Now, this right here," Jerry said, "this would be a great place for a socially inappropriate joke. Does anyone wear a toupee . . . or perhaps recently lost a loved one? Either will work. My wit is versatile."

"Too soon, dimwit," George whispered.

"That's it, George. You're not getting my vote for leader. In fact, I'm voting you out of the elevator."

"Please do. I quit!"

The elevator shifted, a *pop* and a grinding sound piercing through the box. Marcus rose to his feet, the sudden adrenaline swirling his light-headedness into quick vertigo. His eardrums pounded at the foreign noises invading from outside the elevator—outside the place his anxiety had dictated to be his coffin. He gripped the handrail as he felt the elevator's momentum and watched the display numbers countdown to one.

The door opened, sluggish at first, then quick.

Marcus shielded his eyes against the fresh light streaming through the lobby.

Ted, the building's super, stood in the threshold, a radio and toolbox in his hands and a smug curl in his upper lip. "So, you're the bunch who stole my elevator."

"You can have it back," George said.

"Sorry about the inconvenience, folks. Sometimes this old thing has a mind of its own, ever since the upgrades." Ted stepped aside, motioning toward their exit.

"Well, it's been fun, kids," Jerry said. Both he and George wheeled their luggage into the lobby and headed for the exterior doors. "George, you want to get ice cream at the airport?"

"Definitely," George said as they walked away.

Jackson held out his hand toward Ellie. "Look, I'll make the reservations for dinner with your parents. And tell them they should stay with us, not at a hotel. They should . . . feel welcome."

She grinned wide, taking his hand and interlocking her fingers with his. "Sounds perfect."

As they left, Suzette rose to her feet, and she glanced at Martin one last time before leaving. "Thanks for the company," she said.

He nodded, unsure what to say despite a million words racing in his head all at once. A million chances to speak exactly how he felt in the exact moment he felt it, to share with another human being the thoughts in his mind that he usually kept guarded. He tried, but held back. That felt safer.

She smiled anyway, quick and polite.

All alone, Marcus left the elevator. He breathed in the fresh, sweet open air, and wandered past the lobby chairs to the daylight beyond. Strength replenished through his body with each freeing step. Suzette stood in front of the building's glass entry doors, balancing on her high heels but not moving forward. She clutched the postal box, her gaze at the fragile label next to her name.

Marcus paused, waiting, but not for Suzette to step aside. Instead, he searched for the right words, a second chance that still felt foreign and complicated and . . . "You're welcome," he said, his throat dry.

She turned. "What?"

"You're welcome. You know. . . for when you said thank you for my company."

"Oh . . . good."

"Can I help you?" he asked, surprising himself. "With your dog?"

This time her whole face eased with a genuine smile, as if a weight lifted from her shoulders and allowed Suzette to breathe again. He could almost see the burden slip away from her mind, as if melting snow on a spring day. "Thank you," she said.

Marcus took the box from her hands, the hairspray aroma meeting his nose though it didn't sting as much as before. He cradled the box against his chest, protecting the entrusted case as if he were a pallbearer.

As he held open the glass door for her to exit, he glanced at his watch. *Twelve minutes.* They'd been stuck in the elevator for roughly twelve minutes and some odd seconds. Twelve minutes that felt like a lifetime, and yet, he was still in one piece—not perfect and certainly not cured, but still moving forward.

Twelve minutes. Marcus glanced back through the lobby. The elevator sat still. Open. Empty. Waiting.

He studied it, thinking.

"Is everything okay?" Suzette asked.

Marcus hesitated at first, then nodded as he contemplated her question. "Yeah," he said. "I . . . think it will be."

The elevator door closed with an innocent bell chime. This time, there was no groan.

"Thank heavens," she said. "I could use a good day."

Marcus smiled to himself as he followed her through the glass doors. "Me too."

2

MAGICIAN

E.B. WHEELER

"Whoa!" my toddler says,
pointing her chubby finger like a wand
and infusing the world with magic.

A drooping, weather-weary tree
sheds dying leaves.
She runs through,
and they become a blazing orange trail
crackling beneath our feet.

A hedge of tattered roses,
leaf edges crisp and brown, jealously open tissue-paper
    petals
and waft perfume
when she presses her nose in.

A rusted truck,
puking diesel fumes into the air,
rattles the ground.
Her wondering stare
transforms it to a mighty mechanical beast.

A cold, gray pebble,
one among many,
glints and sparkles
as prized as any diamond
when she holds it in the light.

My little girl's wide blue eyes
find magic everywhere.

3

THE CALL HOME

KATHY DAVIDSON

My airship *Hannah* bounced in the wind as Jake, the pilot, eased it to head into the currents.

"That's right." I held on to the rails to keep from crashing around the cockpit. "Steady as she goes. My call should only be a few minutes."

Jake held to the wheel as another gust of wind tried to turn the *Hannah* around. "I'll do my best, Captain."

"Thank you." The ship rocked a bit but hung steady in the sky in the sweet spot that would let me call home: the one stable part of my life. And I needed stability right now—literally and figuratively.

The wireless frequency crackled with white noise and an occasional plip of someone rolling by. "Calling Charlie, are you there?" Charlie usually sat by the wireless, waiting for someone to talk to or listening to the chatter. "Calling Charlie, this is Debbie."

Only static.

A sick feeling dropped my stomach. Someone had to be there

to answer. The airship bucked in the current, and I steadied the radio. Jake couldn't keep us here indefinitely.

A pop and then a clanking sound came over the speaker. I smiled in relief.

"Hello, Hello? Debbie are you there?" With a tap, the frequency cleared up and her voice came through as clear as the June sunshine.

A giggle rolled up in my throat. Maggs was there, my anchor.

"Hey Maggs. How's it going?"

"Doing great. It's good to hear your voice. You sound like you're next door, like I could run through the yard and you'd be sitting in your kitchen sipping your tea."

A twang of something went through me. Was it guilt? Longing? Regret? I didn't have time now to analyze it. "It's good to hear your voice, too."

"Are you close? You could drop by and have dinner with us. I would love to see your airship."

I cleared my throat so my words could come past the lump. "No, Maggs, unfortunately, I'm not close. We found a sweet spot where the frequency is perfect."

"That's wonderful. All those fancy calculations make my head spin. Are you moored to a tree like last time? That was funny. My grandkids got a kick out of that.

"No, we're between the Jet Stream and another wind. It keeps us floating in one place while I talk." I wanted to say something about the ache in my chest—about Sarah—but it wouldn't come out my mouth. "What's new with you?"

"We've been so busy. Charlie doesn't even have time to sit and listen on the wireless. Who knew doing you a favor while you ran off for a few items at the fish market and found your adventure would lead to me starting a business? It gets crazier every week."

I leaned back in the chair. "I hope it isn't too much of an

inconvenience." My worries melted with the sound of her voice, and I let her prattle on.

"Oh, dear me, no. I was getting just as bored with life as you were. Your advice about not growing too fast has been helpful, but we have a waiting list two pages long. We're working as hard as we can on the list of things we have to do before we can add more people. We love it. It's been so good for our family. Hannah loves the work, too. It's just what she needed. Last Sunday, I couldn't find her, and she was over in the shed rolling silverware into the napkins. She always complains that she needs a day off, and then she works anyway. It's good for her to have something to do. Well, for all of us to have something to do."

"I hope you're paying her."

Hannah used to clean my house when I worked and would get so excited when I would give her some money. I always gave Maggs more on the side.

"Of course, I am. What do you think, I'm a slave driver?" Maggs huffed.

If I didn't know my neighbor of nearly forty years, I would have thought she was mad at me, but that's just the way she was. We were closer than sisters, if I had a sister. I laughed at her instead. Trying to decide if the twang was me feeling sorry for myself. I shook my head and moved on. "She likes the job then?"

"Loves it. You know, she always loved to clean up after I cook. Everything has to sparkle. She gets so much joy out of making the dishes and dish covers shine." Maggs' voice beamed with pride. Her daughter Hannah has Down Syndrome. She'd been a happy little girl, so lovable. Now in her thirties, it wasn't always easy to find things to interest her. "You should see her dress the neighbors down when they don't leave their dishes out for her."

Maggs laughed, but I knew she was embarrassed.

Confrontation wasn't her strong suit. It was good she had Hannah to stand up to people. This new food business wouldn't work if the dishes didn't come back. Their motto was, 'Home cooking on plates like home.'

"So, the shed and the steam compressors are working out?"

"I love them. The new ovens finally came and hooked up without a problem. You should see them, Debbie. They're beautiful and shiny. I can cook five pans of lasagna at once in one oven, and in half the time. It's spectacular. And then I still have a whole other oven to toast the bread. They're better than the school kitchens. Thank you so much for offering the steam to me. It was the best."

"You're welcome to it. Henry and I never use it." The thought of Henry made my heart twist a little; maybe I was homesick.

"Well, we use it. I think we are out there in your backyard more than we are home now. It's wonderful. I don't even know what is going on with that soap opera I used to watch, and I don't care. Hannah has stopped talking about the actors as if they were her real-life sisters, which is wonderful. I was getting to worry about her sanity." Maggs was quiet for a second, and I almost found something to say before she got personal, but I was too late. "Have you talked to Henry recently? It looks like he got another haircut."

I took a deep breath. She needed to know, as she was taking care of him for me. "I miss him. I tried to contact him yesterday, and like usual that darn automatic message came up, *Can you call back later?* I swear that man still doesn't know I'm gone. I thought he would notice I was missing after the first few months." I was pretty sure I didn't succeed in hiding my hurt.

"Does he still do that thing where if you don't talk for a few seconds, he pretends the line has been cut? 'Hello, hello? Are you still there? I guess not.' And logs off?" Her impression was right on. She even had his tone perfect. I guess she heard him say it often enough.

We laughed together. I'd rather do that. "No, he tells me if I'm done talking, he has work to do."

"Is his airship getting any closer to being done?"

"It has to be. He has been building it for two years. It's ironic, isn't it?"

Her sweet laughter came through the wireless, and I wanted to hug it. "It is! He's taking all this time to build an elegant airship so you two could travel the world, and you went out and bought a used one and started the adventures without him."

That last comment bit me, and I tried to ignore it.

"His excuse for building such an extravagant ship was to make me happy. Mostly he's putting in a big galley. Isn't that a rage?" I clicked my tongue.

"He probably thought you wouldn't have anything to do if you weren't cooking his meals every day."

We laughed, but it was so sad. I hated cooking and therefore was bad at it. In all my travels, I still loved Henry more than any other man. He put up with my dreams and helped me build my business at the expense of his own. But we grew apart, he in his inventions and me in my business. The ache twisted in my heart, and I didn't want to deal with it. "Has he ever caught you bringing his dinner every night?"

"Oh, he did once." Maggs took a deep breath. "Didn't I tell you about that?" She didn't give me long enough to answer. I was happy to let her tell her story. "I was just slipping the hot plate into your oven when he came into the kitchen. It startled me and I fumbled the dish around and burnt my hand. He ran over to the sink to help me put it under the water, that's when he realized it wasn't you and he nearly fell on the floor. 'Where's Debbie?' he roared. It took a minute for both of us to calm down and for my fingers to stop burning. I just said you were running an errand and had called me because you were running a little late. 'She's not back yet?' 'Nope' I said, wondering if this time he would realize you haven't been around for a while. But no. He smelled the dinner and took it from me. 'Oh, okay,' he says. Like it was no big deal. I can't believe that man still hasn't figured it out. He didn't even thank me for dinner."

"I'm sure he appreciates it. He always got excited to eat your food. I once told him you would give me cooking lessons, and he said it was about time. He's probably happier with our arrangement and pretending he doesn't know." So many emotions flash by: guilt, longing, anger. I settled on feeling numb.

"I still can't believe it's been going on for nearly a year. You've gotta love him, though, right?"

There was a clatter on the other end before I found an answer, and I could hear Hannah demanding to talk.

"I have money to buy new pants." Hannah always loves new pants. She couldn't care less about getting new shirts or shoes; she just likes the pants.

"That's great, dear." I can admit I miss Hannah's sweetness terribly. "But don't forget to get a new warm sweater for fall. It might be cold cooking in my shed this winter."

"It's never cold in your shed." The clatter of the mike hitting the floor told me Hannah was no longer listening at the other end. She liked to talk but she lost focus quickly and wandered off, happy to have been part of the conversation for a moment. I was always afraid to have kids of my own. I wanted a successful business. But here I sat wishing Hannah was my child.

I was grateful when Maggs came back to change the direction of my thoughts. "Sorry about that. I thought Hannah would talk to you longer, and I had to check on the ovens. Make sure the rolls weren't burning."

"You don't trust them?"

"They're new. I'm still figuring out how they work. I think I'll have to rotate the pans to get the rolls to cook evenly."

"How many people are you cooking for now?"

"We're up to two hundred." The shuffling sound of paper came over the mike. "Although the waiting list haunts me. I want to take on the people and make sure they're all eating well."

"What is the next step?" Great, something I was good at and didn't have to think hard about.

"To get more manpower and then put in another steam boiler to run a big dishwasher so Hannah can have her days off. Charlie needs more help delivering food when he gets home from work. We have a schedule of about forty meals every thirty minutes. Charlie doesn't get his food until about nine o'clock. Then he gets up early to take Hannah around to pick up dishes. My other kids are figuring out a way to come help out."

"That's incredible! Charlie might have to quit his job so he can help full time." In such a short time, Maggs built a business. A feeling of pride started to push the hurt from my heart.

"We've thought about that, but we need the insurance. He can't retire for five more years, and who knows, maybe by then you'll be back." Her hopeful voice told it all.

If Henry missed me like that, I would come home in a minute. The twist in my stomach did a little loop. Maybe I felt regret.

"Micha, my grandson, comes and helps after classes, but he's so tired. I promised him he could come help after his university classes are over in a few weeks."

"Our little Micha is big enough to be at university?"

"Oh, yes, he'll be seventeen next month. He's doing well with his classes and wants to be an inventor like Henry. I've been thinking about having Micha bring a few of his friends with him. Delivery and pick up are the hang-ups right now. And his mother, Carleen, is in negotiations with her boss to go part-time so she can help cook."

"It's good they live close enough to help."

"They have always been a help. I love having them. Ben and his family are waiting for the business to get a little bigger, and they'll move home to help. He has already taken over the finances, and the company is doing much better. I'm glad you suggested it. I can't pay much yet, but we need the manpower. The other kids are waiting to see how long the business lasts before they jump in and help. This has been such a blessing."

"Ben is doing well with his family then? I remember all the trouble you had with him."

"Oh, yes. He was my trial. But I think we're the closest because of our struggles. I could never give up on him. I had to love him."

"Because he's family." It was something we always said when she would come to my house in tears because of his struggles. Those times were sweet, and I cherished them. 'You gotta love him. He's family.'

"Yes, exactly. I wouldn't trade him in for anyone. I wouldn't trade any of my kids, or in-laws or grandkids. It's so great. I have a built-in work force. And the blessings still keep coming. Did I tell you Sherry is expecting? They had such a struggle and are finally excited about something."

"That's great. Someone to replace the one they lost."

"Oh, my dear. We can never replace our Krissy. She was so sweet and even though she didn't live long, she will always be part of their family."

I never met their Krissy. I knew they all mourned her as much as they did the death of Maggs' mother. It was a little strange to think I never saw the baby, and I was sorry I missed the funeral. The twang came again, and I changed the subject. "I'm so proud of your success."

"What did you think, just because I had five kids, I couldn't run a business?"

"Oh, I know that running a family like yours was a busy business."

"That's right. This is a cinch after feeding and chasing kids around to all their activities."

There was a long silence. It has always been awkward to talk about having children around me. I chose to have a career. It was a good one, and I was able to sell the business and retire about the time her kids started leaving home. That's when I learned to appreciate her kids coming home and visiting and expanding. My business expanded, but never came home to visit or send Mother's Day cards. The twist tightened, and I had to tell myself to breathe.

"How is ..." I couldn't think what else to say, but I wasn't ready to let the conversation end. Thankfully I didn't have to, because Maggs started talking about the same time.

"So, tell me where you have been lately. What exotic ports have you visited?"

"We left Taiwan this morning with cargo for a place in Mexico. My new man Carlos has a nose for what will sell there. So far he has been right on and we are making progress."

"That's great. So, Carlos is working out, even though you don't know much about him?"

I laughed. She was right. The man was quiet and kept to himself. He was a wiz at purchasing and selling. But I was afraid his glare intimidated the buyers into not negotiating. After what few words he said about his past, I wasn't sure I wanted to know more. "He's really harmless. I've had no trouble, and he is pulling his weight."

"And you gotta love him."

"He's family," we said together. Maggs was my best friend and had a deep understanding for people. It was a comfort.

"What else is bothering you?"

"What?"

"I can tell there is something bothering you or this call wouldn't be as long."

The lump in my throat kept me silent for a moment, but I swallowed it down.

"Sarah is leaving."

"Oh, Debbs. I'm so sorry. She's been with you since the start and is an excellent engineer, keeping all your engines running."

"Her father is sick, and she's going home to help her mother."

"Do you think she'll come back? You've gotten so attached to her. She's your family."

"I know. She has family she has to look after. What can I do about it?"

"They're her parents. Of course, she has to go help them. You have done so much for her. She was so broken when you found her, and you were there to help her and give her a safe space to heal. You did something no one else could do. You gotta just love her."

"How can she do this to me? After all I've done for her?" The anger leached out in my voice.

"She's family." Maggs got me to say it with her, and I could feel the twist lessen a little.

"I'm so sorry, Debbie. I wish I could give you a hug right now." There was a clatter at the other end.

Hannah's voice boomed through the speakers. "I got red pants. They look like the sauce in the lasagna, so people can't see when I spill."

"That's a great idea," I told her through my tears.

"Sorry about that." Maggs came back.

"Don't worry about it. You're lucky to have Hannah."

"Yes, I am. I love her more each day. I couldn't imagine my life without the little snipe."

"Give her a hug for me. And Charlie and Micha and all the rest of your family. They are a treasure."

"Yes, they are. And don't worry, you'll find another engineer."

"Yes, I will." I had to swallow twice to get my words past the knot in my throat. "But it won't be the same."

"It's never the same. But you have to love her and be happy for her. If she sees your anger, she is less likely to keep in touch or even come back for a visit. Don't be afraid to show her how much she means to you."

There was a bit of a silence. My throat tightened again and I couldn't swallow it away. How was I supposed to let her go? The airship shook with the turbulent wind currents.

Jake yelled from the cockpit, "Captain, the Jet Stream is moving. I can't hold this position much longer."

Time to go back to work. I pasted a smile on my face and buried my hurt. "Gotta go, Maggs. Thanks for talking to me."

"Of course. You're family. No matter what anyone says. My kids still call you Aunt Debbie. Come home anytime."

"Thank you." There was so much in my heart I could never be able to express to Maggs. "Goodbye."

"Take care. Goodbye." Charlie and Hannah chimed in to say goodbye.

I listened to the white noise until Jake yelled from the cockpit. "Sorry for the interruption, Captain, but the wind is pulling us back into the Jet Stream."

I gathered myself together, trying to deal with the hurt and anger. It wasn't Sarah's fault she had to leave, and I really did want to see her again, even if she never came back. I walked out to the cockpit and stood beside Jake. We watched the clouds below in silent companionship. I knew he'd miss Sarah, too. That twist came again, and I realized it was because I had a new family, and I wasn't sharing them with Henry. He would love this life. I should have told him where I was going. There could still be time.

He might still love me. I was his family.

"Head into the wind. Let's get Sarah home." And maybe visit home ourselves.

4

SPRING WHISPERS
ALICE M. BATZEL

At last, long-awaited sunshine
and warmer temperatures.
Snow melts.
Warm rains awaken lawn and ground.

Small green sprouts shyly peek,
foretelling tulips, daffodils, and crocus.
Brave pansies shed silence and
courageously speak with spontaneous bloom.

Birds venture out, hop on wobbly legs,
flap winter-weakened wings, and chirp in delight.
With newfound strength,
they claim the ground, tree, and sky.

Gardeners refresh yards and flower beds.
Yards get a good raking, brushing, and aeration.
A hearty fertilizer nourishes
lawn and garden soil.

Voices of man and nature once again
resound outdoors.
All speak of anticipation, faith, and hope
in the promise of a season of new life.

Young and old, strong and infirm,
embrace renewed joy and vigor.
"Come and see!
Spring whispers, 'I am coming. Surely, I am here.'"

DARK

"Deep into that darkness peering, long I stood there, wondering, fearing, doubting, dreaming dreams no mortal ever dared to dream before."
-Edgar Allan Poe

5

PITCH BLACK
MIKE NELSON

I lurched to a stop, unable to see anything. LED headlamps don't just fail, but mine had, and it had quit at probably the worst possible time. I was nearly an hour inside a dangerous, hard-rock mine. And I didn't have an extra light.

There is nothing as dark as the inside of a deep cave or an old mine. I fought to control my panic. My body wanted to bolt but couldn't. Doing anything besides standing very still and collecting my thoughts would be dangerous.

I'd been in old mines a lot. They intrigued me. I'd explored dozens of them over the years and had often found antique treasures left behind by the miners. One wall of a cluttered room in my basement was filled with old miner's lanterns, rock drills, and other abandoned hand tools. The opposite wall sported floor-to-ceiling shelves filled with minerals that I'd found while kicking around in the old mines.

None of the minerals were worth much. They were just *fascinating*, and that was okay with me. I didn't go into the mines seeking fortune. I just liked old miner stuff.

Hoping the batteries had failed, but instinctively knowing

they probably weren't the problem, I knelt on the rocky floor in the inky blackness and fumbled in my backpack. I took several deep, cleansing breaths in a vain attempt to drive away the debilitating panic that lay just beyond rational thought. My eyes had become utterly worthless. It didn't matter whether I opened them or closed them. I saw nothing.

Even though a loud ringing filled my ears in the black silence, I could hear water dripping that I hadn't noticed before. I became acutely aware of my raspy breathing and my thudding heartbeat. The clammy coldness of the air around me raised gooseflesh on my arms, and the pungent scents of mildew and rat droppings punctuated the choking odor of freshly-disturbed dust.

I recoiled at the thought of rats. Although I didn't fear them per se, just the thoughts of being there in the dark, possibly surrounded by swarms of the bulgy-eyed, hairy creatures, started playing with my sanity. I frankly couldn't wrap my mind around how a rodent could see any better in the blackness than I could, but they were there. I could smell them. Worse yet, rats attracted snakes—one of the rat's natural predators—but I doubted any self-respecting snake would have probed that deeply into the mine—or would they?

I don't like snakes. I am perfectly okay with them, as long as I see them first, but snakes don't speak—except in tales of witchcraft and magic. Very few even offer a hiss or a warning rattle unless you're about to step on them. More often than not, they just lie there—waiting.

The thought of snakes brought back a vivid memory. I'd come across a hibernating ball of rattlesnakes in a hole not far inside an old mine early one spring. They didn't move much because of the cold, but the sheer mass of all their shining, scaly bodies lying twisted altogether in that dark, dusty hole still haunts my dreams.

Realizing I was letting my imagination run wild, I pulled my thoughts back to the task at hand and stirred through my pack, finally locating my extra batteries. My light uses two, so I always carry six just to be safe. Truth be known, though, until that moment, I'd never opened that baggie.

A prickling sensation crept up the back of my neck as another thought crossed my mind. What if the batteries had aged out? They were supposed to be good for ten years in storage. But what was storage, anyway? Was it a closed cardboard container sitting on a cool, dry shelf in the storage room? My extra batteries had been bouncing around in my backpack, possibly for years. In all that time, my pack had been hot, cold, damp, jostled, crammed with treasures from the mines, and often mistreated.

I tried to calm my racing mind again. Even if one or two of the batteries had a problem, surely there would be two, out of the six, still serviceable. Then another thought defeated that conclusion. All six batteries had probably come from the same original package. What if I had a bad lot? What if ...

I fought again to control my thoughts. I had to get and stay calm. Wild thoughts this early on in my dilemma were not only counterproductive but possibly dangerous.

Then another thought crossed my mind. The idea had been there since my light went dark. Batteries never suddenly fail. They ordinarily fade slowly away, allowing one to stop and replace the weakening batteries before the light went out. Such wasn't my case. One moment my headlamp had been filling the rocky shaft ahead of me with bright light, and in the next instant, I'd been plunged into pitch blackness.

I fumbled a couple of batteries out of the baggie and sat down on the floor. Now I had another problem. Not being able to see how the batteries were oriented in my light, I had to use my sense of touch to determine how the slim AAA batteries went into the light. Worse yet, I couldn't remember whether or not the battery box lid was attached to the light or if it might come loose and drop into the rocky debris on the mineshaft's cluttered floor. If it did, I'd probably never find it again in the coarse gravel.

Ever so slowly, I felt for and found the battery cover and pushed it first one way and then the other until it finally opened. A calming feeling swept over me when I realized the lid was hinged and permanently attached to the light. I carefully found the ends of the old batteries, felt the slight nub on the positive end, and then slipped a newer battery into each slot and reclosed the cover.

The moment of truth was at hand. I pressed the rubberized on-switch, expecting to see a sudden burst of light. None came, and my horror deepened.

I carefully reopened the battery box and inverted the battery orientation to satisfy my fears that maybe I'd gotten it wrong the first time. The results were the same.

I had to fight my emotions again as I fumbled two new batteries out of the baggie and slipped them into place. When the results were the same, again, I methodically inverted the batteries, hoping—no praying that I'd somehow mixed up the negative/positive orientation. Nothing worked.

I muttered dark, low curses into the silence around me, naming the company that had built my headlamp. I knew now that the electronics in the light, and not the batteries or the tiny LED lights, were at fault. One or two LED lights might burn out over time, but my light had ten! I frantically pushed the rubberized switch, again and again, hoping by some strange coincidence that I might somehow reconnect the broken connections. I even slammed the light against the palm of my hand several times, hoping to jolt the loose or broken contacts. Nothing worked.

Refusing to panic yet, I stuffed the useless light into a side pouch and mentally traced through the rest of my pack's contents. I had an old, metal 35mm film canister full of strike-anywhere matches, somewhere. There were probably only a couple dozen matches in the container, but at least they would light my footsteps for a few more precious minutes as I raced back towards the mine's entrance. I carefully considered that thought. I'd been wandering in the mine for over an hour before my light quit. Matches had a finite life. I'd probably need a case of matches to find my way back out.

Then I considered the rest of the contents of my pack. All else failing, I could set fire to my spare shirt and use it as an improvised torch.

I found the matches without much effort, collected and stowed all my loose gear, picked up a small rock to use as a striker, and got to my feet.

The first match flared, driving back a respectable bulge in the inky darkness. Then panic nearly overcame me again. I was standing sideways in a horizontal shaft hewn out of the solid rock by the ancient miners. I couldn't remember which way I'd been traveling when my light went out!

I thrust the burning match near the floor and searched for footprints. There were none. The shaft floor was strewn with sharp, rocky shards the miners hadn't bothered to remove, and what little dust lay over the scattered gravel was too fine to hold and reflect a footprint. I raised the match to chest level and searched in vain for any distinguishing marks on the walls.

The flame burned my fingers, and I dropped the match, instantly plunging the shaft around me into total blackness again.

I instinctively turned around, facing what I was convinced was the way out, and began shuffling along the wall of the lightless mineshaft. I pressed on without striking another match for a while. I needed to conserve what few I had left. I remembered coming across three offshoots from the main shaft on the way into the mine. I had piled up loose rocks in a sort of rock cairn to mark each of the shafts that I had chosen not to follow. My hope now was I could find the cairns when I came across the offshoots.

The crunching gravel beneath my feet cast haunting echoes off the stone walls around me as I walked. Suddenly, without warning, I bumped headlong into the side of the rough-hewn shaft, nearly breaking my nose in the process. I thought that strange at the time, the tunnels were less than eight-feet wide, and I thought I'd been traveling parallel to the jagged walls. Assuming I'd just gotten disoriented in the blackness, I held my arms straight out to my sides from that point on so I'd be sure to walk parallel to the walls.

Other thoughts began to haunt me as I ambled along. I'd come into the desert alone, which was nothing unusual. My friends weren't particularly interested in old mines. Most were claustrophobic or more interested in other, more normal pursuits of recreation—like golf. For whatever reason, I hated golf.

I soon realized just how dumb that was. If only I'd brought a buddy or a brother, we'd have at least one good light between the two of us. Even better, I should have had the foresight to bring along a spare light!

Caves and old mines were always chilly, and as such, I didn't carry much extra water with me. Now, though, my mouth and throat were parched, dried by my heavy, panic-stricken breathing. I had two plastic, twelve-ounce bottles with me. I stopped to sample a little water from one, wetting only my mouth and throat, knowing I needed to conserve what was left.

All sense of time and distance fled as I shuffled along. It felt like I'd been walking for hours. Surely, I should have found the entrance by now. Yet I knew at the snail's pace I'd been making I couldn't have traveled very far from the point where my light quit. On my walk into the mine, I'd strode confidently along, watching only for abandoned tools, interesting mineral formations, or hazards—low-hanging ceilings, rock falls, or fissures in the main shaft. Now my confidence had fled. I wasn't even sure if I was moving toward the mine's entrance or if I was walking ever deeper into the black bowels of the mountain.

I lit another precious match from time to time in a vain attempt to recognize something—anything that would tell me whether or not I was at least making some progress. Each time as the match flared and then finally dwindled, I could see no change in the jagged stone walls around me.

I suddenly stumbled over what felt like a large rock. Until now, the shaft's floor had been relatively uncluttered. I regained my balance and reached out with my right foot. My blood ran cold. There was more than one rock. I'd been walking for what seemed like hours, and now I instantly realized I'd been walking in the wrong direction. There hadn't been a rockfall in the shaft before now.

As I stood there trying to calm myself, my heightened senses detected the soft but unmistakable flow of cool air. I decided to sacrifice another match to see where it was coming from. The instant I struck the tiny flame, the cool breeze snuffed it out. In those brief milliseconds, though, like a quick flash of light through a camera lens, an image flooded my brain. A stark white pile of boulders blocked my path.

I stood still for several long moments. Not only did the soft, cold, dust-free breeze continue to flow over my face from the direction of the rock pile, but now I could also hear the distinct pitter-patter of falling water. It wasn't a roar like an underground stream, just the soft splashing of water into a shallow pool.

I knew I had to turn around and go back, but I was intrigued by what I'd seen. Until now, the mineshaft had been hewn out of a dark rock, probably ancient limestone. What lay ahead of me appeared to be quartz. I wondered if that's what the miners had been following when they blasted this shaft into the mountain. A seam of pure quartz often encapsulated gold ore.

Although gold was the last thing on my mind, I knew it was only a matter of time before I found my way out of the mine, and then what? The mine hadn't seemed dangerous or threatening before my light failed. I knew I would want to come back and find the quartz again.

I fumbled in my pack for my spare shirt, tore off a sleeve, and knelt on the floor, facing away from the breeze. It took a few moments to light the fabric, and when I turned around this time, the light from the flaming sleeve instantly told me several things. First, a large mound of pinkish-white quartz lay directly in my path. Second, the shaft I'd been following had suddenly ended in a wide, dark fissure. Water dripped from several places in the ceiling, much of it cascading unheeded into the dark cavern beyond my eyesight. Several smaller rivulets splashed down into shallow pools on the fallen quartz.

When I held up my puny torch, I could see that the shaft's ceiling had collapsed, leaving a large, black, empty hole above. I wondered if the quartz had fallen into the tunnel before or after the ancient miners blasted into the cavern and abandoned the mine.

The breeze intrigued me. I remembered reading an article about airflow in underground caves. Airflow could come from fissures in the mountain, or it could come from the ebb and flow caused by atmospheric pressure changes outside the mine. By measuring the airflow, scientists could roughly gauge the size and volume of the cave.

I couldn't see any ambient light filtering through a crack leading to the outside world, so I assumed that what lay before and below me was a deep cavern leading down into the black bowels of the mountain. A terrifying thought swept over me. I could imagine demons lurking in that bottomless, black cavern.

As the flames on the lighted shirt sleeve dwindled, I spotted a hand-sized shard of rose-colored quartz lying near my feet. Deciding it would make a perfect addition to my home collection, I picked it up and slipped it into my pack. Then I turned around and jogged back down the shaft behind me while the dying torch still lit my way.

Although I now had an even longer journey ahead of me, I knew one thing. I'd be headed out of the mine and not ever deeper into the belly of this pitch-black pit.

When the last flames of my makeshift torch began to burn my fingers, I dropped the smoldering fragment and hurried forward until total blackness folded around me again.

When I could no longer see, I fished the film canister out of my pocket and felt the remaining match heads inside. My heart sank. I only counted six precious matches. On the bright side, I still had most of a shirt to burn. Time, though, was of the essence. I needed to get out of this black hole—the sooner, the better.

I knew when I lit another *torch*; I could run while I could still see and then deal with the blackness again when I couldn't. I knelt on the floor and tore my shirt into six rough pieces. Then remembering how the flames had burned my fingers, causing me to drop the precious remnants of my last torch before it completely flamed out, I pulled out one of my plastic water bottles. I didn't want to drink all of its precious contents right then, but I needed a handle for my torch.

I methodically sipped all of the precious water, stuffed the first piece of the shirt into the mouth of the empty bottle, and shouldered my pack. Then I struck match number one of the remaining six and held it to the fabric. When the material finally flared, I raced off down the shaft. Ahead, the dimly-lit, rough-hewn walls bracketed my flight. Behind me, the icy breath of blackness, possibly filled with unspeakable demons chasing me from the bottomless pit in the mountain, drove me to run even faster.

Just as my makeshift torch began to smolder and die, a dim sight ahead brought me to an abrupt halt. The single shaft I'd been following split into three separate tunnels. In the blackness I'd wandered through before, I hadn't even noticed the splits. As the shirt remnant flamed out, I dropped to my hands and knees and frantically felt around on the floor in each of the three branches, looking for one of the rock cairns I'd left behind. There wasn't one. Now, I was perplexed.

I got back to my feet and stood silently, considering my dilemma. Before I lit another torch, I forced my mind into a string of rational thoughts. By doing so, I immediately dismissed the shaft that turned ninety-degrees to my left. I hadn't noticed any branches in the tunnel while I was erroneously fumbling my way ever deeper into the mountain. That left two other possibilities. I had kept to the left wall on the way in, so now I assumed that if I followed the shaft to my right, I'd be moving in the right direction.

I lit torch number two and scrambled down the dim shaft on my right. As I hurried on, I saw features I hadn't noticed before, and I worried. The shaft meandered, following slow bends here and there that I hadn't noticed while I was inching my way along in the darkness.

The miners had probably been following a vein of ore when they pushed the shaft into the mountain. I smiled at the irony. Why couldn't the vein simply have gone straight into the solid rock? It would have saved everyone, including myself, a great deal of time and effort.

When the torch flamed out, I lit torch number three and jogged on. I began to doubt again. I hadn't been in a hurry before my headlamp failed, so I would have thought, now that I was jogging, instead of walking, I'd be nearing the entrance.

I suddenly pulled up short. Another rockfall blocked the tunnel ahead of me. My decision to turn right at the junction had been horribly wrong! I spun around and ran back the way I'd come until torch number three died, and I was swallowed again by blackness.

I leaned heavily against the rock wall and tried to catch my breath. The panic that I'd felt when my headlamp first failed returned. What if the middle shaft I'd ignored at the junction wasn't the right one either? I couldn't imagine I had come out of the right-angled tunnel without noticing the hard bend to the right, though.

I stood for long moments, trying to estimate how far I'd run down the wrong shaft. Finally, after forcing some measure of calmness over myself, I lit torch number four. This time as I ran, an urgency I hadn't felt before swept over me. I could feel the icy breath of the demons chasing me again. If I failed to find and choose the right path this time, I could be trapped forever in this utter blackness, not knowing which branch in this maze of tunnels to follow.

My adrenaline-laced flight pushed me faster than I'd have ever imagined it would. Moments later, I recognized the three-way junction again. Without even pausing to consider my plight further, I selected the middle tunnel and raced on.

By the time torch number four burned out, I was exhausted and slumped to my knees. Deep in my subconscious mind, I fought a battle. I'd been lost in the forest once, many years before, but even though panic had driven me then, as it did now, at least I could see where I was going. Now, my only perceptions were sightless eyes, burning lungs, aching legs, and an ever-present, grinding fear, knowing that nobody knew where I was.

That thought brought me up short. I hadn't told my wife, Becky, exactly where I was going that day. For the most part, I never figured that out myself until I was in the hills. I was so far out in the desert this time, though, that it might be weeks before someone stumbled across my truck. Once they found my truck, it wouldn't take long to find the mouth of the mine and start looking for me inside, but I didn't have weeks. At the very most, considering what little water I had left, I had a couple of days or so before …

I couldn't face the truth.

I slowly got to my feet and struck my fifth match. By the time the torch finally flared, I was on a dead run again, assuming this time I would soon see the light of day. This time as I raced along, I was confident. I could no longer feel the icy demons behind me. My lungs and leg muscles burned, but those were both good signs. It meant I was still very much alive, and hope was pushing me on.

When torch number five flamed out, another insidious thought crept into my mind. I distinctly remembered building three rock cairns on my way into the mine, and once I'd turned down this middle shaft, I hadn't come across another branch. That thought forced a deep nagging doubt into my reasoning. Had I sped right past yet another offshoot, or was I in the wrong tunnel again?

Sweating profusely, I decided I needed to cool down. I unbuttoned my shirt and pulled it off, leaving my back naked to whatever breeze might have been following me. I needed reassurance. I needed—hope.

Then, I realized I could no longer feel the breeze flowing from within the mountain's bowels. Afraid I was perhaps mistaken; I turned around to face the tunnel behind me.

I felt nothing! There was no breeze. Something was terribly wrong! If I were headed towards the opening, there should have been a breeze. I pulled my shirt back on and struck my final match.

Horrified, I watched as the flame on the match head sputtered and died before the final scrap could catch fire.

Screamed curses echoed off the cold, unforgiving stone walls all around me. At first, I barely recognized my high-pitched voice. I wasn't one to curse without reason, and even when I did curse, the words didn't flow out of me in an unending stream of expletives as they did now. A thought crashed through my otherwise out-of-control mind. I felt sanity, as I'd known it, slipping away.

I suddenly fell mute. Without being able to reason, I was doomed. A flash of foreboding crept over me, and I swear I could see the specter of my rotting corpse lying face down in the gravel, surrounded in the impenetrable blackness by a soft fuzzy horde of feeding rats.

I had to press on or die.

Then another thought crossed my mind. The last rock cairn I had stacked in the side tunnel entrance had been on my right. I had to calm myself and methodically find my way out. I didn't have any other choice. I moved to the left side of the tunnel so I wouldn't miss the branch in the dark, felt the cold rock with my hands, and stumbled on.

Time ceased to exist. My only sensations other than the crunch of gravel beneath my plodding feet came through the fingers of my hands as they scraped along the jagged tunnel wall.

I began to feel dizzy. I'd had an ugly bout with vertigo years before, but an inner ear infection had brought that on. Then I remembered what a forest ranger had told us on a guided tour deep inside a cave in the mountains. Vertigo was a real thing to fear in total darkness.

When I became too dizzy to stand upright, I dropped to my hands and knees and crawled on.

Dizziness and nausea swept over me, and I vomited what little life-giving water I still had inside me over the coarse gravel between my hands. Then, even unable to maintain a crawling position, I lay down flat in the gravel.

For a long time, I lay there, feeling my body tilt and heave as my mind fought to decide which way was up and which way was down.

Then another chilling thought came to me. I remembered

bumping headlong into the shaft in the darkness. That wouldn't have happened unless ...

The memory of the right-angled shaft I'd dismissed at the three-way junction before glowed brightly in my mind, and I faced the unbearable fact that I had once again been following the wrong tunnel. No wonder I couldn't feel the soft, cool breeze flowing toward the entrance! If I had only thought to stop and pull my shirt off at the junction before I swept through it, I would have felt the breeze and been led toward light and freedom on the outside.

Memories wafted through my mind like a summer breeze, memories of better times, of loved ones, of life on the outside.

Knowing I had to find the right-hand bend before I could make yet one last push for the entrance, I struggled to my hands and knees, lowered my head, and crawled on. Once again, I lost all concept of time and distance. My knees and the palms of my hands burned from dozens of tiny cuts caused by the sharp, blast-fractured rock that cluttered the mine's floor.

I didn't want to quit, but I needed to rest.

I lay down again on the jagged gravel, planning to rest for just a few moments.

Much later, a soft fluttering sound forced its way into my slumber. At first, I just lay there, confused.

Then, suddenly I recognized the soft sounds—bat wings. At first, I recoiled in horror. I hated bats, almost as much as I hated rats or snakes! Then I realized that the tiny winged creatures were probably headed out of the mine to feed on insects.

Suddenly knowing I needed to follow them, I struggled to my feet and held my arms out to my sides to keep from slamming into the walls and stumbled on. But eventually, the fluttering horde left me behind.

Refusing to surrender, I fought back the dizziness and nausea and pressed on. Then I stumbled and fell across a pile of fallen rock. A faint breeze tousled my sweat-soaked hair. The soft sounds of pattering water filled the air around me.

Horrified, I realized where I was. The bats must have been returning to their roost in the deep cavern lying just ahead of me. I must have slept through the night and then followed them back into their lair in the bowels of the earth when they returned before the morning light.

I refused to panic. I reached out towards the patter of splashing water. At least I wouldn't die of thirst. With water, I could live for days—perhaps weeks. Maybe someone would eventually find me. Maybe when night came again on the outside of the mine, I could follow the bats out. I wondered, where they lived in total darkness, how they knew the difference.

I lay down in the gravel to rest. My head swam. My body seemed to tilt at weird angles. Nausea overwhelmed me again, and eventually, I faced the inevitable. I would not be able to stand and follow the bats when they headed back out of the mine, and I couldn't crawl fast enough or far enough to follow them out. Unless someone came to my rescue, I would remain here, trapped in the pitch blackness.

Then I heard it. It was little more than the soft crunch of weighted footfalls on gravel, yet it was there. I struggled to sit up, rested my back against a boulder, and watched for the reflected light of my rescuer. Just as I drew a deep breath to call out to them, a soft huff echoed down the stone corridor. I was not alone.

6

NIGHT FRENZY

ALICE M. BATZEL

A consuming fire burns within me.
Another night's chronic irritation,
unrelieved nor calmed by medication, meditation,
or self-analysis. My detested relentless companions,
sleeplessness and discontent,
force my surrender. I leave my bed and yield
to a compulsion to free this thorn.

The city outside my door sleeps.
An overhead light shines dimly upon my kitchen table.
Thoughts seep slowly from my brain to arm,
hand, pencil, and finally paper.
Words first creep through a fissure in my head.
A breached dike in my mind gives way.
Unrestrained gushing thoughts escape.

I write page after page for hours.
My hand aches, cramps, and spasms.
Pencils dull. Unrestrained voices liberate
dialogue and story upon stacks of writing papers.
I am driven to weariness, then to exhaustion.
My hand, now a limp, misshapen, swollen claw
of gnarled knotty joints can give no more.

The first hint of dawn dares to bleed
over the horizon outside my window.
A chaotic trail of frenzy testifies to my night hours.
Countless dulled pencils sprawl across the table.
Writing papers strew and heap upon one another.
Be it madness, I question. I know not, only that
they witness my many restless nights.

First light of day spills softly into the room.
Moment by moment, the sunrise illuminates
the battlefield on my kitchen table.
My skin warms, and strained eyes yearn to rest.
I see the truth of my many fitful nights.

7

WHERE CRICKETS SING
DEDE MATTIX

Martin had awakened on his sixth birthday to find himself held captive in the arms of his dead mother. She'd wrapped him in her feverish, wasting embrace every night for months, but in the end, it had been sudden cardiac arrest, not the cancer, that took her. Martin's child-mind couldn't comprehend her overnight transformation into a rigid monster. Rigor had formed her hands into claws that would not release him. At first, he'd shut his eyes and whimpered, then finally screamed until he was hoarse. By the time the hospice nurse found him at eleven—after stepping over the drunken father passed out in the hallway—young Martin had been catatonic.

These were the memories that paraded through Martin's mind now, precisely one hour before his alarm was set to go off this Monday morning. It was May first, his fifty-eighth birthday and the fifty-second anniversary of his mother's death.

A day he would do his best, yet again, to forget both.

He'd startled awake to a strange sensation he'd never experienced before—an ominous presence snooping around inside his mind. There'd been no gradual fading of his usual pragmatic dreams, nor the normal mental calendaring of his work week. No, this day his ever-present fear of death had apparently embodied itself as some mental entity, probing and pushing his thoughts about. Oddly enough, the invasive sensation took him back to his youth, watching his Uncle Sef with one arm up to the shoulder inside one of the family's Holstein cows, grappling with the misaligned limbs of a calf.

Martin felt as though the cobwebs of his dreams were pushed aside by a freakish knowledge as unyielding as cast-iron.

Death would come for him this very day.

For a moment, fear lurched in his chest like a panicked horse. Then he calmed himself with a sensible reassurance. He was far too young to die. He was just four years from retirement, and his physician had only recently pronounced him in excellent health. But the more he tried to reassure himself, the faster the fingers in his mind simply moved the awful pronouncement back to the forefront of his considerations.

Stella snored away on her distant acreage of the bed. Martin would not wake his wife with this ridiculous mental charade. He'd simply face it and prove it wrong. She would certainly be more concerned about a change in her bridge club refreshments than his alarmist notions, anyway. Like Halley's comet, her orbit seemed retrograde to his; their time of actual connectedness had long since passed.

As he showered, he thought of their estate, nicely settled. The wills were in order, the summer cottage paid off. Their only child, Bob, was a continent away getting his PhD. They barely even heard from him. Thanksgiving dinner, when he chose to show up, was a short and rather torturous ordeal. And as for Christmas, it was clear Bob would rather spend it skiing in Aspen while Martin and Stella nursed martini's and stared at their TVs in separate rooms.

Martin took care to leave the bathroom tidy, as always, and

followed the aroma of coffee downstairs to the kitchen. Stella had already laid out the business section of the paper beside his toast and jam before scuttling off to her end of the table to brood over her horoscope. It was their morning routine. Coffee instead of conversation. Marmalade rather than matrimony.

He pitied her thinning hair, skewered with curlers and pins, and the sallow jowls and cupped eyelids filled with rheum. She was absent-mindedly drawing over and over the same penciled star beside Virgo's reading for the day, and it was as if Martin was already gone—for all the difference his presence seemed to make.

Martin finished his coffee in silence and left.

When he was halfway to the train near the corner of Second Avenue, a piebald puppy bounced out from behind a hedge, lolloping up the sidewalk towards him. Martin waved it away, but it insisted on following and nipping at his heels. Then, just as the city bus lurched into the gutter, the pup dashed right in front of it. There was a shrill yelp and a brief flash of black and white as it went under the tires.

Aghast, Martin stumbled away from the crimson pavement towards the commuter train. He could almost swear he'd seen a curious iridescence flicker above the pup as it convulsed and died. Looking back once more as he boarded the train, he shuddered for the second time that morning.

It was a portent. Death, up close and brutal on this of all days.

Neither the overheated train nor a second round of coffee at the office could warm the chill that had seized him. His secretary, Miss Mims, gave him a concerned look over the second cup.

"Everything alright this morning, sir?" she asked.

He merely nodded and set to work. Clearly the morning's stressors had come from restless sleep. A good round of catching up would set things right. By noon, his stack of completed work was quite satisfactory and his mood markedly improved. When the usual lunch crowd gathered at the elevator, Martin smiled at Miss Mims as if there had never been a smoother morning.

As they entered The Suede Mandolin, Martin's eyes were immediately compelled to a loud, portly man dominating a crowded table near the back of the restaurant. Though a total stranger, the man nodded and raised his glass meaningfully in Martin's direction. Martin was discomfited by the bulging eyes and lingering gaze following him as he continued along to his own party's table.

Martin found himself transfixed by the argumentative man now glistening with sweat. So much so, that Martin's own soup cooled and his sandwich went untouched. Around the room conversation rose and fell, and his coworkers scarcely noticed his distraction. Suddenly the man arose and pounded a fist on the table. Then, turning an enigmatic eye towards Martin, he slumped to the floor.

Restaurant patrons stood in alarm. One bent to feel for a pulse in the paunchy neck. Emergency personnel were summoned, but as the pasty, corpulent body was trundled past sometime later, Martin had a certainty the others did not. That same curious iridescence had shimmered above the man as soon as he'd hit the floor. Whatever had animated him moments before had fled, and all the medicine in the world would not restore it.

Martin did not eat his lunch.

Once secluded again in his office, away from the belabored retelling of the lunchtime drama, he sat before his desk and felt a tremor deep in his bones.

Supposing all this was real, after all?

What could possibly be the point of having a precognition of one's own day of death?

Who would even believe him if he was foolish enough to try to tell it? And what was he supposed to do with this supposed knowledge? Try to make right every wrong in his entire life? Try to reconstruct in one day a marriage that had taken decades to dissolve? Call up a son who clearly didn't want a relationship with him? Or merely keep it all to himself and simply leave a note in a sealed envelope ensuring his computer passwords were left behind?

Martin was not a particularly religious man, but he rather supposed that prior to this day he'd likely had the world divided somewhat when it came to his understanding of death. There were those who became ill or seriously injured, and thus were granted by the Fates a time to meaningfully set their affairs in order. And then there were those poor unfortunates who, he'd always believed, had no warning whatsoever---perhaps they went down in a doomed airliner, fell under a bus, or ... toppled over their prime rib in a fine dining establishment while brokering a deal on an exceptional piece of downtown real estate.

But what if he'd been wrong? What if each of them had actually been wakened before the break of dawn, given a personalized warning, and then left to deal with that imperative as they saw fit? What would he have thought if the shoe had been on the other foot, and Stella had wakened him with such an absurd story? Most certainly he'd have scoffed and blamed it on too much sushi the night before.

Besides, he had no meaningful proof that this premonition was real. Why should he believe it? Just because he couldn't shake the fingers in his mind, that knowing sense of certainty. Or because he'd watched a dog get hit by a bus, and a fat man choke in a restaurant? He could chalk the entire thing up to his freakish paranoia of death, and all of it happening today, on the anniversary of his mother's death. He'd never lived a day of his life since then without fighting the image of those clawed hands at his throat.

Angrily, Martin snapped open his desk drawer to search for

a file just as Miss Mims stepped in and handed him the day's mail. There was only one letter, but somehow, he knew the sender even before he looked. It was addressed to himself and postmarked Ohio. The letters came unfailingly, persistently, despite the fact he'd never once answered his cousin's invitations to come back to the farm to visit, to bring Stella and young Bob. All these years had passed, even after Uncle Sef and Aunt Becky had passed, and still the patient invitation was pleasantly extended. There was always a chatty letter updating him on news of the extended family—extended family which Martin admitted to himself he was secretly curious about.

Reluctantly, he opened the letter, and out fell an old photo of the big white barn he'd tried so hard to forget. There was Uncle Sef holding a prized calf in his arms.

Suddenly, it seemed Martin was no longer in the overheated office of Pembrooke and Stiles but hiding miserably behind that old barn, and he was a thin twelve-year-old boy. He was hiding from Uncle Sef, ashamed to face him. After watching Uncle Sef reach for hours inside a cow dying in labor, Martin had been sent to hobble a young heifer to foster the orphaned calf. But he'd been too hasty, too eager to please. The spotted heifer came falteringly when he poured the oats, rolling her eyes at the hobbles. Perhaps it was because Martin's hands were shaking or still slick with amnion, but he'd failed to latch the hobbles fully. When the orphaned calf was brought in, the spotted heifer had lashed out with a wicked hind foot. The hobbles had snapped, and the newborn was hurled into the stone wall. It was the second death of the night, but this time it had been Martin's fault. In shame, he'd fled into the woods.

Later, after his uncle had gone to the house, Martin had stumbled from his hiding place.

He'd felt numb when he looked over at the body of the dead cow, covered loosely with a tarp.

He stood over the dead calf lying in the straw and stared at the congealed blood that had drawn a mask of grotesquerie over the delicate baby face. Martin drew one booted foot back and kicked at the calf with all his might, again and again. Then, he fell to his knees and wept over the body, laying his head on the soft hair of the ribcage.

It was Uncle Sef's two strong hands that had pried him away at last, using the same soothing words he'd spoken to the dying cow through her delivery. "There, there. Let me hold your pain. Let me hold it."

For a time, Martin had felt as if his insides were jelly. Then came a burning shame at having cried like a sissy, so that when Uncle Sef extended a clean hanky, Martin had flinched away.

Uncle Sef's words had surprised Martin. "You've a home here with us, lad. I'm sorrow at what alcohol has done to your father—"

A sudden fierce loyalty for his father had pulsed through Martin in a boiling red wave. It eclipsed his shame, even eclipsing the yearning for comfort he'd felt in that home. For a moment, he thought of how even though he'd holed up in his room every evening as the family played card games, they'd cajoled sweetly at the foot of the stairs for Martin to come join them. Yet he'd lain stubbornly alone in the dark and tried to focus only on the way the crickets orchestrated their night music on the same precise beat. Then, thrusting that yearning from his mind, Martin stood, teetering, and filled with his puny rage.

"I hate it here!" he'd shouted. "And I hate all of you! I want to go home to my father."

He remembered the look in his uncle's eyes. Not hurt. Not even anger. Only compassion.

How could that man, who looked so much like Father, behave so very differently? All those weeks Martin had spent on the farm, the gift of that summer, Martin had received nothing but endless affection from Uncle Sef. How could Martin have been expected to make sense of those two worlds—the misery of the cramped apartment where he'd lived with his angry father, and that world of sudden warmth and laughter, where for those few weeks he'd been invited to visit?

That day in the barn telescoped away, gone as suddenly as it had come and carrying with it the scent of rain-washed countryside and the pattering drips of rain falling from the eaves. Martin was sitting in his chair in his office. The letter and the picture fell to his lap, and he realized moisture had gathered at the corner of his eyes.

Why had he gone back to his father?

Back to the beatings, the silence, the poverty, and the shame. Uncle Sef and Aunt Becky had taken him back to his father that very night, packing a box with some extra clothing and homemade goodies which his father had later thrown into the dumpster behind the gas station up the street.

And Martin had gone that night to his chilled bedroom and cracked open his window, listening in vain through the chaos of city noise for the soft sounds of the crickets twining together their soothing, perfect melody.

As he stood now before his desk, he realized it was already time to go home. There were streaks of rain on the office window, and he thought about how it had rained on the night he'd left that warm country kitchen where a loving family had set a place for him and invited him in, offering a world of acceptance and love.

And he thought of standing at the kitchen window of his father's apartment that same night at midnight, watching his father out on the cold porch with a bottle of whiskey, rough-shaven and miserable. And Martin knew.

He knew now and realized in some way he must have known even then.

He'd come back because Uncle Sef and Aunt Becky and Jeffrey and Rachael didn't need him; they had each other. But his father was all alone. And so, Martin had come back for *him*.

Two tears tracked down his face, perhaps the first two since that night staring out that apartment window silently watching the suffering man on the porch.

Martin turned, blew his nose, and straightened the papers on his desk. He called and had flowers sent to his wife. He wrote a brief thank-you card to his cousins, leaving instructions for Miss Mims to see that it was delivered. He called and ordered a fine bottle of sherry to be sent to his son, along with a note expressing pride in his many accomplishments. Then, with a poignant smile, he wrote his computer passwords and tucked them in an envelope and put it at the back of the top drawer of his desk.

Martin nearly missed the train home. He squeezed aboard just as the doors were about to close. A curiously buoyant feeling seemed to have settled upon him, his first inhalations of life untainted by guilt or shame. He wondered half-heartedly if he should have called a cab—but perhaps the cosmos had prearranged the outcomes regardless of his choices. He tried to feel some angst, to work up the grudge he'd carried all day, but no—the effervescence lightened his body, seeming to erase years from his joints. He felt a slight, ridiculous smile tugging at his mouth.

It was extraordinary.

Something was happening.

He wondered if it showed. He glanced around, but the other commuters were absorbed in their own little seashell worlds. A waitress was tallying her tips for the day. An elderly woman worked away at a knitted cardigan, spilling it partially over the lap of a student busily reviewing flashcards. Only a young Asian mother, cradling a sleeping child on her lap, stared back at him.

Suddenly it occurred to Martin that death might not just be about him today.

What if it was about the other passengers, too? That sleeping child?

He stood, abruptly. His briefcase clattered to the floor and several pairs of eyes turned Martin's way.

He wanted to warn them, but the words wouldn't come. He tried to speak, yearning towards the Asian woman with her child, but the effervescence in his chest surged until he wondered if he might actually be floating upwards from the floor. The surge swelled and he leaned into it, feeling his face beginning to contort as if G-forces would grapple it apart and stretch his features into a great oblong void. There came flashes of ivory at the edges of his irises, which spiraled into great streams of light, canted chronicles of other times and places he unexpectedly remembered:

The smell of the nursery before his mother became ill. The discovery of a blue glass bottle in the sand at Chelsea Bay. His hand reaching out to pet a pony at the fair, and the same hand flinching as a teacher struck him with a ruler. Rice sliding from his collar as he undressed on his wedding night. Stella with her flowers in the garden. Watching his small son through the chain link fence of the elementary school yard. The affair he'd almost had. His father's funeral.

The memories pulled and separated.

Single letters plucked at his skin; vowels stabbed at his eyes, becoming clustered nonsense that strove to free itself from the small frames of syllables. Diphthongs and digraphs, clauses and conjunctions sheared into each other in a great iambic shudder as all his years flew through him. The words became moths, the sentences appeared to be bats that began a frantic flapping, deafening his ears so that when at last the scream began, he did not even hear it.

It seemed to be Martin's own dying scream, his own telling at last. But it was also the scream of metal twisting metal, the overthrust of railcar into railcar at the speed of demons summoned from hell. As bodies and shards of glass spiraled towards him, the scream rose upwards towards its highest pitch until it swung finally upon its own acoustic axis and wound itself back down into an unexpectedly soothing anthem.

It was an anthem Martin seemed to remember, the gentle undersong he'd been seeking all along. The lost letters and vowels streamed back around him, re-twining the scattered syllables into what had for so long been unspeakable. It was love that washed over and through him as he came to rest in a familiar and comforting place, where, if he was very still, Martin was quite certain he could hear the song of crickets match the fluttering symphony of his own pulse dwindling faintly in his wrists.

8

LEATHER LANTERNS
BETTI AVARI

We are naught but leather lanterns
Vessels of light we shine our brief patterns
Stitched with sweat and stains and tears
We glow for days, or months, or years.

Every light begins the same
Fed on dust and moth and flame.
Sinew and vein the wick we weave
A flash, a flicker, a steady beam.

We all take and also give
Both the soft and garish light—
The warmth that others too might live,
And the flash that gives a fright.

The paths that we illuminate—
Filled with love and filled with hate
—cross over viscous magma cooled
Galactic dirt that's trod and tooled.

To each glow we give a name
But no flame is ever quite the same.
Of life and death are certain patterns
For we are naught but leather lanterns.

LIGHT

"It maybe that you are not yourself luminous, but that
    you are a conductor of light."
-Sir Arthur Conan Doyle

9

THE UFO
VALERIE ODENTHAL

Our class raced for the windows the second we heard the shouted announcement of an unidentified flying object on our elementary school's playground. A real UFO!

We were the same children who had heard JFK announce that a moon landing was a national goal. Our parents worked for the company that made missiles, booster rockets, and "all things space." Other parents were involved with the air force base nearby. Astronauts, NASA, and rockets, were part of the fabric of our entire community. Naturally, we assumed that if there was an alien encounter, we would be in the center of this meeting.

Behind the glass, wide-eyed students scrambled for a peek. Questions about communication with other worldly beings left us with a sense of wonder. Saturday morning cartoons had us believing in little green men from Mars. Talk of space monsters from B-grade movies caused panic in young imaginations.

And here was our very own UFO.

Even our teacher was ready to participate in this historic adventure. She marched us in line outside onto the blacktop. All the classes joined together as would-be scientists. There it was. Wrapped around the flag pole—a large blob of iridescent bubbling fabric the size of a love seat, flapping in the wind. The custodian was trying to free the thing from a tangle of ropes, flag, and the pole.

When the emergency crews showed up to help in the rescue of our UFO, we knew we were a part of history. Still not sure what we were witnessing, whispers about little aliens continued in clusters of huddled students.

"It is a wayward weather balloon," our principal announced.

Back to our classes we marched with questions about weather balloons, UFOs, and science, one question spilling out over another from the flock of alien fans. We wanted to know everything. So, an impromptu lesson on science, weather, technology, wind speed, and who has to collect all of that data filled the rest of our afternoon. Later, a group of scientists came to collect their lost balloon.

Still, we were not entirely convinced that they weren't secretly collecting aliens before we could glimpse the historical landing right there on the playground. Even though our Unidentified Flying Object was now identified, we still wanted it to be from outer space and not just the local weatherman.

To this day, *what if* questions still lurk in our minds.

10

FIRST WINTER DAYS

ALICE M. BATZEL

Gray skies silence autumn.
Harvest sheds bulge
with tiller, weeder, and plow.
Waxed paper packets hold favorite seeds.

Cool temperatures awaken us in the morning.
Frost dusts the last blades of grass.
Cold blowing rains speak of what is to come.
Snow gently falls.

Quilts and blankets pile high atop beds.
Coats, sweaters, caps, hoods, toboggans, scarfs,
heavy socks, and boots stand ready
to armor body, head, and feet.

Cold winds whistle. Hot cider soothes our shivers.
Soups and stews simmer on home stoves.
Fruit cobblers bubble in Dutch ovens.
Yeast bread bakes in loaves.

Lingering apples cling to orchard branches.
Birds scavenge for winter berries.
Rumbling thunder shakes the ominous dark air.
A squirrel scampers for final gathering before his long
sleep.

11

IMPERFECT INSTRUMENTS: A THREE-PART HARMONY

E.B. WHEELER

"This is going to be your only helicopter ride. Too bad you can't look out the window."

I didn't understand why the guy thought I'd never go on another helicopter. Of course, I also wasn't sure why I was on this one. My head was strapped to a backboard, and I had a hazy memory of trying to unbuckle my seatbelt and not being able to move my arm. Of firemen peeling the top of my car open like a tin can. Otherwise, the day was black.

I opened my eyes again. The room looked like a hospital— white walls and fluorescent lights—but I couldn't remember how I got there. A blond nurse leaned over me.

"Have you ever had a back injury?"

"Yes," I mumbled. "I might be lying." I couldn't find the energy to explain that I'd been thrown from a horse and hurt my back a few years ago, when I was still in high school, but the injury hadn't been serious.

"We're going to do an MRI. It may take a while."

"Can I sleep?" I had a vague idea that people with head injuries shouldn't sleep, and my head didn't seem right.

"You can sleep." They moved me into the glowing metal tube, and I slipped out again.

I hung in a drug-induced slumber while the doctors tracked down my parents and told them to expect the worst. My neck and back were broken in three places, and my brain was bleeding. I probably wouldn't pull through. If I did, I might be in a vegetative state. I almost certainly wouldn't walk again.

One of my only waking memories was of the LDS missionaries giving me a blessing. I don't know how they found me. Maybe it was because of the CTR ring the nurse cut off my swelling finger. I also don't recall much of what they said, except for two things:

You will recover completely.

Don't give up your musical pursuits.

I sit at the piano, my hands hovering over the keys. I know the song. I've had it memorized for years. This isn't to say I'm a talented musician, but I love music. There's something satisfying about pounding your happiness or frustration into a keyboard. Now, my fingers curl into my palm, the muscles wasted, my hands almost skeletal. Muscle memory lingers. My fingers twitch, wanting to reach out, but they feel like they're tied with rubber bands. The song is still there, but I can't give it voice. I slam the lid closed and limp away.

There are times I'm angry with God. Times I want to shout and cry and throw things. I feel deserted. But no matter how angry or lonely I feel, I never quite stop believing in Him.

The neurosurgeon picked tiny fragments of splintered bone out of my spinal cord. He took bone from my hip, shaped it, and replaced the broken vertebrae, joining the pieces with titanium plates and screws.

I was conscious more often after the surgery. Bruises purpled my face and my abdomen from the seatbelt, and my nose and throat were burned raw from the chemicals in the air bag. I thought I couldn't move my leg because of the surgery on my hip. I thought I'd be able to move my hands again when I got my strength back. I had faith in that blessing.

About a week after the surgery, I asked for crackers and juice —the first thing I'd eaten since the pancake breakfast before the accident. The doctor and therapists came to talk about what would happen next.

"I'm going to walk in my graduation at BYU, then my best friend and I are going to Europe," I rasped out in a faint whisper.

"We'll see," the doctor said. I didn't understand her uncertainty.

They fitted me for a body brace—a contraption of metal bars, straps, and padding that locked my spine into alignment—and made arrangements for physical rehabilitation.

I've often thought, if I could go back to the morning before my accident and do one thing (other than warn myself to watch out for the soft shoulder on the highway), I'd play the piano one more time. Piano isn't my favorite instrument, though. Violin is. Unfortunately, I never got past "Twinkle, Twinkle Little Star" and other classics of the screeching-cat school of beginner violin. It might be just as well, because I can't imagine how much losing that would have hurt.

Each Christmastime, I dust off my violin and scratch out "O

Holy Night," my favorite carol—the one song I'm determined to learn, no matter how bad I sound. One year, perhaps a decade after the accident, my husband congratulated my efforts by saying, "That's getting a lot better. I could tell what song it was."

The *Book of Mormon* talks about being an instrument in the hands of the Lord, a force for good in the world. I try. But if God wants me—any of us—to do His work, I sometimes wonder why He doesn't give us better tools. It's hard to make beautiful music with a broken instrument.

One of the nurses checking me into rehab laughed good-naturedly at my wispy voice. "Sounds like your singing career is over."

I smiled and pretended it didn't hurt my feelings. My singing career, which involved a bit of musical theater and church choir, was sinking like a rock. To protect my spine, the neurosurgeon went in through the front of my neck for the surgery, and in the process he accidentally cut the nerve that controlled my right vocal chord. My throat would heal from the air bag's chemical burns, but my voice, supported by just one functioning vocal chord, was an airy whisper, and I didn't know when or if it would recover.

My rehab neurologist introduced herself and did some tests, gently poking my skin with a pin, using both the sharp and dull ends to see how sensitive my nerves were.

Left side first. Sharp. Dull. Dull. Sharp. Dull.

Then she did the right side.

"I can't feel that," I whispered.

Her smile faded. "What about this?"

"Maybe a little pressure."

"Sharp or dull?"

"I don't know."

She had to do some reading, but she came back with the diagnosis: Brown-Sequard Syndrome. The shards of bone that had sliced my spine didn't sever my nerves completely, but they'd shotgunned my spinal cord. I had areas all over my right side—mostly in my abdomen and leg—where I couldn't feel anything, and muscles in my left side—especially in my hand, arm, and back—that would waste away to almost nothing. Because the patches of paralysis affected all four of my limbs, the neurosurgeon handed down the verdict of quadriplegic. I was stunned. Cold. But God promised I would recover completely. The doctor had to be wrong.

———

I need a musical outlet, and I believe God means for it to be part of my recovery. Music has a healing power that sometimes transcends even the abilities of drugs and other therapies. It can't heal a broken spinal cord, though.

Still, I'm drawn to the idea of music therapy. The harp is considered the ideal instrument for therapy work. Therapy harps are not the stately instruments you see playing with the Tabernacle Choir. They fit in your lap and weigh under ten pounds.

The deep notes resonate in my chest as I cradle the instrument against me, and even my wasted fingers can pluck the strings. Best of all, there's nothing to compare it to. I never considered playing the harp before, so every note is a new triumph.

Plagued by self-doubt and hungry for hope, I devour writings that help me feel like God hasn't forgotten me. An article in the 2005 *Ensign* by Elder Glenn L. Pace, "Confidence and Self Worth," gave me a jolt. He wrote that the Lord can use our weaknesses to bless us and bring about good in our lives. I had thought of weaknesses as something to overcome or be ashamed of, but I had never considered that what I think of as weaknesses and shortcomings may simply be those circumstances that put me where I was supposed to be—the place where I can play my part in the symphony of life. I don't know if that's always true, but it's a reassuring thought, especially when my burdens weigh me down, and I pray for them to be lifted, and the only answer seems to be silence.

The days in rehab were brutal and boring, sometimes at the same time. Physical therapy is abbreviated PT. That really stands for Pain and Torture. The therapists worked us until we cried, until we threw up. Not only girls cracked under the torment. Grown men and teenage boys sobbed unabashedly. Once, while I was sitting on a mat with tears running down my face, a man in a wheelchair rolled by and said, "At least you can still feel it."

Speech therapists ran endless tests and computer analyses on my voice, which registered almost too high for the human ear. My voice had been replaced by a dog whistle.

The worst day of the week was when I had to go in for counseling. The psychologist never smiled.

"You need to set new goals for when you leave," she said.

"I'm going to get back into music." I'd gotten a refund on my tickets to Europe. I didn't consider it a betrayal of my faith, just an acknowledgment that God doesn't always work on my time frame.

"You need to accept that you can't do the things you used to do."

"I'm going to play music. Play the piano again."

"I had a patient who loved music. After his spinal cord injury, he had someone tape drumsticks to his arms so he could tap on the drum."

I was horrified on the kid's behalf, though maybe he didn't feel sorry for himself. "I don't want to play drums."

The best part of the week was when volunteers came to sing and play guitar for us in the evening, the music soothing away every other thought.

The only problem I have with the harp is that it's so sedate. The remaining muscles in my hands are stronger from plucking the strings, but no matter how hard I pull on them, I still get a gentle, mellow sound. There are times I need to be loud, to jam my frustrations away, especially when my body won't do what I need it to.

One of my favorite scripture verses is Isaiah 40:31: "But they that wait upon the Lord shall renew their strength; they shall mount up with wings as eagles; they shall run, and not be weary; and they shall walk, and not faint." Sometimes I feel like I've run as far as I can, and then I spend a lot of time waiting.

The doctors oohed and aahed over my recovery, but I wasn't satisfied. My left foot still hung lifelessly, and I couldn't move my left hand. My therapists talked about making adjustments.

They ignored my insistence that I was going to get better. I was grateful for what I had, but I believed God when he told me there was more to come. I had a feeling that on a particular day coming up, my fingers would move again. It was my lifeline. I clung to it.

When the occupational therapist came that day, all businesslike, I couldn't stop grinning.

"I moved my thumb."

"What?" He gave me a skeptical look, maybe thinking he'd misunderstood my whisper.

"Look." I held up my wasted hand and moved my thumb up and down. It was a tiny movement, hardly more than a twitch, but it happened under my control. The therapists warned me that once muscles are paralyzed, even temporarily, they never recover completely, but I rode on a spiritual high. God hadn't forgotten me.

I told them that my foot was going to regain movement, too —I was going to recover completely—but they still fitted me for a brace to support my paralyzed foot so I could learn to walk again. The day they brought my new brace in, I wiggled my big toe. I think they were actually a bit annoyed, after all the work they'd put into making the contraption I would no longer need. By the time I left the hospital, I was able to walk a little, and I even made it to my college graduation, clutching my cane and terrified the whole time that I was going to fall and get trampled by the hundreds of other graduates. But I walked. Things were going to keep getting better.

The harp is a great step for me, but it's not taking me all the way to my goal. I start looking at other instruments—delving deeper into the world of folk music with its array of beautiful, unusual sounds—and discover the hammered dulcimer. It consists of paired strings laid out across a soundboard and struck with wooden hammers. Like the piano, it's a percussive string instrument, suited to bluegrass music and folk tunes.

My husband, a talented woodworker, builds one for me. It's hard to remember when I've had more fun making music. One of the tricks to playing it is to have a loose hold on the hammers so they have some bounce to them. My fingers can't grip anything tightly anyway, so I pound away at the strings, getting some great bounce, and the harder I hit the notes, the more energy goes into the song.

It's even better than piano. Not as pretty as violin, but more loose and fun. I've wondered if I ever would have discovered it if I hadn't lost those other instruments.

A story in the *Book of Mormon* has gained new significance to me since my accident. In the scripture, the prophet Nephi and his family are traveling through the wilderness, dependent on hunting for their survival. Their bows wear out, and Nephi's bow—the best one they have—breaks. Everyone's upset with Nephi and with God. But Nephi makes a new bow and prays. God shows him where to find food, and the family is happy again. The thing that stands out to me is that Nephi didn't feed his family with his best bow. He did it with one he made himself in the wilderness. He didn't need the best instrument. He just needed persistence and faith.

Free from the watchful eyes of nurses, I practiced walking at home. First from one couch to another. Then down the hall. Then around the house. I still limped, but I set my cane aside.

The worst problem was my voice. People could hardly stand

talking to me because it was so airy and squeaky. When I told the speech specialist I'd planned to be a teacher, he winced and described adaptations that would allow me to speak, though I'd never have a normal voice. I walked out of his office with my weak foot dragging, wondering if I needed to find a new direction in life.

Then the bishop of my church congregation asked if I would be the chorister.

"Really?" I squeaked. "I can't sing. I can't even talk."

"I know," he said. "Will you do it?"

I was already embarrassed by all the attention I got because of my body brace, which I would wear for several more months as my neck fusion stabilized. The idea of standing in front of a congregation of my peers and showing off my weaknesses—my inability to talk or sing—made me cringe. But my mother had raised me with the idea that you don't turn down a church calling, so I agreed.

Picking out the songs gave me something to do that week. I wished I had a more complex calling, something to fill my hours besides PT exercises. There wouldn't be much to the assignment until Sunday came around.

The night before my first Sunday as chorister, I took one of my walks around the yard. It was cool, pleasant, and stars were bright overhead—a perfect evening. It reminded me of one of the songs we were singing for church the next day, "How Great Thou Art." I took a deep breath and sang, "O Lord, my God, when I in awesome wonder consider all the worlds Thy hands have made …"

The notes came out perfectly, not even a little bit squeaky. I stopped and stared up at the sky, wondering if I'd imagined it. I tried another song: "How firm a foundation, ye Saints of the Lord, is laid for your faith in his excellent word." Strong and clear. I went inside and said something—I don't remember what. My family stared then laughed and asked a million questions. I could only attribute my recovery to God. The doctors were certain that my voice would not come back, but I agreed to do what the Lord asked of me, and He gave me the instrument I needed accomplish it.

Yet despite continuing physical therapy at an outpatient facility, my progress plateaued. I limped badly. My left hand was so weak I could barely hold anything, and my good hand wasn't much better. I broke a lot of dishes. The therapists declared me healed, but this wasn't my idea of a complete recovery.

I haven't forgotten my desire to play therapy harp, especially given how much I appreciate the people who sang to us in the hospital, but my harp skills will never be more than marginal. Still, when they open a new rest home just down the street from my house and reach out to the neighborhood, asking us to come visit, play the piano, anything to help the people with dementia make it through the difficult evening hours, I volunteer. It's a perfect audience, really. Even if I do terribly, they'll forget by tomorrow.

So I play my little collection of songs. My left hand seizes up, as it often does when I'm nervous, and I end up mostly playing the right hand melody. My audience squirms, fidgets, mumbles.

They're all LDS. I grab the hymnal from the piano and look for something in a key I can play. I haven't practiced these, but I know the tunes. I pluck out the simple melodies, and the residents grow calm. Some close their eyes. One gentleman leans forward, calling out requests.

"You're playing it too slow!" he shouts.

My face burns, but I can't go any faster. When I'm done, my critic is still frowning, but he's sitting back in his chair, his posture relaxed.

"Thank you!" one of the nurses says. She glances at the critic. "I hope you'll come back?"

I look at my audience's peaceful expressions. "Yes, I will."

I'm fortunate to be as functional as I am. A statistical anomaly. A miracle. But I believed I would heal completely. I still hope for it and work for it. I can walk, but because of the imbalance of my muscles, I'm always in pain, except for the spots where I feel nothing at all. Once, I stepped on a toothpick and it went all the way into my foot. I didn't realize it until I noticed the trail of blood on the carpet.

The thing that stings the most is not understanding why my healing came this far and stopped. I got my voice back against all probability, so why not my hands or my foot? Some days my faith feels worn pretty thin. Did I make a mistake and push God away? Did He forget I was here?

I try to have faith that this is for the best. After all, there are things I wouldn't have discovered, wouldn't have done, if my body was whole. When I pray and listen, I feel reassured that there is a reason behind my trials, even if I can't understand it yet. Waiting is more exhausting than running, but maybe only in the times when we are still can we hear the strains of the heavenly music playing all around us. It's a great swell of voices, each as different as piano, violin, drums, harp, or hammered dulcimer, but capable of coming together in beautiful harmonies. I like to think, if I listen closely enough, I'll understand my part in it a little better.

My two pregnancies were nightmares. The stress pushed my muscles and nerves past their endurance, and I spent nearly the full nine months of each on bed rest, throwing up and in excruciating pain every time I got to my feet. But I love my daughters more than I could have imagined—worth every moment of misery.

My second child was a fussy baby, and often the only thing that soothed her was my singing. My vocal range is much less than it once was, my sense of pitch a bit off-key, but she doesn't care. Even now, as a toddler, whenever she's upset, she runs to my arms and asks me to sing. She doesn't demand that my voice be perfect. She's satisfied with my imperfections. I strive for the faith to accept them as well, to trust that God, the Great Conductor, knows how to arrange His orchestra and make beautiful music using imperfect instruments.

Originally published by *Segullah* journal April 15, 2015, https://segullah.org/announcements/contest/imperfect-instruments-a-three-part-harmony/

DARK

"Everyone is a moon, and has a dark side which he never
shows to anyone."
-Mark Twain

12

MY MIND'S EYE

JOSEPH A. BATZEL

I look out this same window each day.
Thoughts race through my mind.
Who are these people who visit me?
Their faces, their smiles, are rarely familiar.

So many questions.
"How are you today?"
"Would you like something to eat?"
"May I help you dress?"

"Not well."
"A sandwich, please."
I can do it.
Clearly, they cannot hear me.

Why is this so hard?
I try to talk, but no words.
I try to laugh, but no smile.
I try to cry, but no tears.

I am trying hard to speak.
Thoughts race through my mind.
I can see you. I can hear you.
My mind is shouting!

Why can't you hear me?

I have a visitor today.
I'm excited. Maybe I'll remember.
He looks familiar.
He calls me "Professor."

Was I a teacher?
What does he mean?
I search for his name.
Nothing.

I think I remember
wearing a shirt and tie to work every day,
standing before hundreds of students,
teaching them how to speak.

The image in the mirror vaguely familiar
Old man wearing baggy pajamas
supported by a walker.

Why can't I speak?

It once was easy to recall names,
dates, places, people, events.
I had the memory of a scholar.
Now, I search to find my name.

Another day, another face.
She says that she's my wife.
But that cannot be, she's too old.
She says, "I love you."

She asks me questions.
"Are they treating you well?"
"Would you like me to read to you?"
"Can I do anything for you?"

I try to answer.
"Yes."
"Yes, please."
"No. I'm fine."

Why are you leaving?
I am trying to remember.
Who are you?

Oh, hello. She's back again.
Same face. Same smile.
Same questions.
Who is she?

I hear a faint voice behind me.
"I'm sorry,"
it whispers.
"He can't remember."

13

SOMETHING SHINY

BETTI AVARI

June Galleo

"Look!" I hold my sun hat with one hand and point in the direction of a glint of light with my other. "Against the cliffs. There's something shiny over there."

Our kids squeal with delight as we hit a wake. I grab for the railing to steady myself as we hit the bump of rough water, and lose my grip on my hat.

I reach for it, but like the end of a kite string in a gust, my hat is just out of reach as the wind carries it over the back of the boat, and it flips and flops down to the water.

"Careful!" Tony calls over his shoulder.

"Too late," I call back. "I lost my hat!"

He looks back at me and the engine slows. "You did?"

"Yes," I groan. "Back there. We have to turn around." As the wake from our boat begins to settle, I can see my sun hat bobbing in the froth. "Quick, before it drowns!"

The kids giggle at my theatrics. Even they know I love this hat.

Tony rolls his eyes playfully. "To the rescue!" he says, spinning us around. The kids squeal again as the boat roars through the tight turn and accelerates.

We slow alongside the lifeless hat. It's barely clinging to the surface tension that keeps it afloat. Tony kills the engine and reaches for a long, hooked pole as our momentum continues to float us ever closer.

"Kids, go sit with your mother," he says as he drops the anchor, kneels on the bench, and extends the pole as far as it can reach.

At seven, six, and four, the kids are quick to obey. They huddle close to me in a giggling mass of life jackets and sunscreen.

"Are we close enough?" I ask. I didn't grow up near the water, so uncertainty is a common emotion for me out here. It's not easy to wait in suspense for news of my favorite hat. "Did it sink?"

He leans over, over, over the side of the boat.

"Tony. . . it's just a hat. I'll get over it if it's lost."

"No, you won't," Tony turns to look at me and rolls his eyes playfully. "You'll scour the entire internet, never find anything similar, and curse me for dragging you out here."

I could've used a long nap instead of a day on the boat, but I'll never tell him that.

"I won't curse you," I sigh playfully. "We both wanted one last outing before the baby comes. And a new hat could be a bonus, even if it is different. I'll just need to find a more current style, that's all."

"A little faith, June. It's a hat, not a top-secret mission. Try to relax," he calls as he teeters over the side.

Suddenly, he falls over the edge.

I gasp. "Tony!"

The boat rocks underfoot as the children and I race to the bench where he kneeled moments before.

I can still feel the warmth from his legs on the vinyl seat cushion as I peer over the edge. The hooked pole is floating on the surface, and a mass of bubbles erupts beside it.

We've been visiting Porcupine Reservoir for years now, and I still feel like a stranger here.

But it's very beautiful. Tucked into a remote canyon, the reservoir is surrounded by aspen banks, rock cliffs, and pine forest peaks, and the picturesque views makes it worth the extra drive. We borrow his dad's boat a few times every summer, and Tony knows how much the water intimidates me, but his playful antics won't be abated, even for my nerves. "Haha, Tony," I growl.

The girls giggle.

"Very funny!" I try to keep my voice even. I'll never get over my nerves, but I don't want to worry the children, either.

He surfaces dramatically, clinging to my rescued hat. He wipes the water from his face, then he growls. "The treasure has been found, matey," he growls in his best pirate imitation.

The kids love it. This begins a string of "Argh, matey!" and "Ahoy!"

He swims to the back of the boat with my hat in tow. "Your treasure, my lady!"

"My hero! And how shall I repay this kindness?"

"Why, by joining me for a swim!"

It's been raining off and on for days, and the air is hot and sticky, so a dip sounds great. Due to the iffy weather and it being a weekday, we're the only people here, so I don't bother hoisting the orange flag. I toss my sopping wet hat aside as the kids jump in.

First is Avery, our precocious four-year-old, her brown curls bouncing as she leaps into Tony's outstretched arms. Then Carmella and Gia jump in while holding hands. We affectionately dubbed them "the twins" because they are only eleven months apart in age. And last, baby Clara, who is due in under two months, joins me for a dip as I gingerly climb down the ladder.

It's a playful ten minutes before I feel the gentle tightening of a Braxton Hicks contraction across my swollen belly. "I'm out," I say. "Tony, can you help me up the ladder?"

He climbs up behind me. "You alright?" he murmurs.

"Just a Braxton Hicks. But I should probably take it easy for a little."

"I'll make it a smooth ride back to the dock," he promises.

I smile. "Liar." I reach for my crumpled hat and press the woven fibers with my fingertips, trying to smooth the brim back into shape, but I worry that it's a lost cause. Tony saved it from decomposing at the bottom of Porcupine, but I don't think it's salvageable; I'll have to do an internet search when I get home after all.

Another glint of light catches my eye from the wooded shoreline. Is someone there? I start to search the glove box for a pair of binoculars when another Braxton Hicks closes in around my abdomen, and I glance at my watch.

Less than five minutes apart.

The boat bobs side to side in a sudden breeze and worry pours through me. "No," I remind myself. "I need to relax." I shuffle to the wide bench and lay down, close my eyes, and take a deep breath. "You're okay," I whisper. "You're safe."

I've never gone into labor prematurely.

I have no reason to worry.

My meditation is short lived. The kids clamber up the ladder and towels and water bottles are everywhere in a matter of seconds.

"Up, up, up!" Tony orders.

I turn my head in his direction and squint as I open my eyes. There's more flashing from the rocky shore. Tony pushes the last of the kids inside, and I sigh. "I don't know how we'll manage four."

"Together," he winks as he climbs aboard, dripping wet, and towels off. "It's weird, but I think I saw a canoe underwater."

"Where?"

"Directly beneath us."

"It's been a weird day." I sigh. "Have you seen something shiny flashing at the base of the cliff? It's distracting."

Tony doesn't answer. He seems preoccupied.

I blink a few times, then close my eyes once more. I focus on the warmth of the sun absorbing into my skin, the gentle breeze caressing my belly where our baby is kicking, the sounds as Tony gathers discarded towels and tosses them into the corner of the boat before he reaches into the cooler for a water bottle.

Through my closed eyes, I can still make out the bright light glinting from the wooded shoreline. "Tony?"

"Yeah? Are you feeling okay?" He plants a kiss on my forehead, then I feel him tense. He kneels beside me and takes my hand. "Another contraction?"

"I *think* they're Braxton Hicks, but they're only five minutes apart. This is the third one." I don't dare to open my eyes. I don't want to see him try to look calm.

He taps his smart watch. "Set a timer for five minutes," he orders. His phone buzzes a response. Countdown. He weighs anchor, then he turns to the kids and claps his hands three times. "One, two, three!"

"And on the seat!" the kids respond. He's trained them well. He always jokes about running a tight ship, but he really means it.

A shadow pours over us as Tony starts the engine, and I press my lips together. The vestiges of pain that had been building start to fade, and I admit to myself that this third contraction was more than a little gentle tightening. These really are contractions. Avery was two weeks early, but I've never delivered five weeks early before.

This is probably a false alarm.

I hear the engine rev, and for a moment I think we're floating in the smoothest water I've ever experienced. Then the engine sputters and Tony curses under his breath as he kills it.

I open my eyes. "What is it, Tony?"

"We're not moving."

"Forget to weigh anchor?"

"Uh, I'm not sure. Give me a second." He kicks his sandals off.

My eyes fly open. Is he going back in? "I was only kidding. I heard you raise the anchor."

"Yeah, I know." He's peeved.

Another cloud overhead blocks the sun. The breeze is picking up, and across the water, at the edge of the pine covered mountains, I can see dark sky through the canyon. "Tony, look. I think we have a microburst forming to the west of us."

He's climbing down the ladder, but he stops momentarily, looks west, and nods. "Two minutes," he promises before he disappears into the water.

Avery whines from the seat across from me. "Mo-om!"

"What is it, sweetheart?"

"Mella and Gia aren't sharing!"

"Ladies? We have lots of popsicles, can you give Avery another one?"

I hear a splash as Tony surfaces. His smart watch is beeping. He turns it off and curses again.

"Tony?" I call. He doesn't answer. The sky is growing darker by the minute, and the breeze gives me a chill. I sit up gingerly and reach for my hoodie under the seat, only to remember I left it in our vehicle. So I put my sundress on, and teeter slightly as I walk to the back of the boat and peer over. "Tony?"

He's holding onto the ladder with one hand, and the other is pressed to his chest.

A mixture of alarm and panic hits me as I focus on his pale face and hunched shoulders. "Tony, what's wrong?"

He looks up at me. "There's, uh, something down here. I think we're stuck."

One second, I'm a butterfly, panic dancing in my veins. A moment later, I'm a rhinoceros, as fluttery fear converts to viscous dread.

"What is it, a log or something?" He wouldn't have grown pale over a log. Despite the growing pain of another contraction, I answer my own question. "Wishful thinking?"

He nods.

"On a scale of one to ten?"

He nods and sets his jaw. "A hundred."

I swallow. On my pain scale, this new contraction is a six. The hot pain intensifies, and I turn away from the water, lower myself to the bench, and lean back. I think the words of our birthing coach as I take a deep breath. *"In through the nose, out through the mouth."* The breathing for stage one of labor.

After another deep breath, the contraction starts to wane. My eyes flutter open and I take in the sight of our three daughters sitting across from me. They're oblivious, playing with their sunglasses on the bench. Innocent. Carefree. As they should be.

I hear Tony surface again. Did I hear him dive? He's blowing water from his face, swimming to the ladder. I look over as he climbs into view. His expression is still one of shock. Dismay. Water is pouring off him as he climbs aboard, but he doesn't reach for a towel. He stands at the back of the boat and holds his hands away from his body at an awkward angle.

"Tony. . ." I don't want to alarm the girls, but I need him to get me to a hospital. "I need to see Lauree Gardner this afternoon." I say my OB-GYN's name like it's the neighbor up the street, as light and unworried as I can possibly sound. It works; the girls pay no attention to me, but Tony does.

He nods slowly and looks right at me. "Any pressure yet?"

"No. But I wouldn't give it more than an hour, maybe two. Should we try calling her from here?"

He hurries to the pile of towels in the corner, grabs one at random, and begins wiping his hands. "Do you have any hand sanitizer in your duffle bag?" He usually teases me about being a germaphobe, but for once he's dead serious.

"Always." I try to grin, but there's no forcing it.

He turns to the girls. "Can you get mommy's hand sanitizer from her bag?"

I point at my duffle. "The front zipper pocket."

Carmella tries to hand the bottle to him, but he reaches his outstretched hands toward her instead, palms in a cupping shape. "Just dump some in my hands, will you, sweetie?"

She obliges, and as she squirts a generous glob into his waiting hands, the container makes a fart noise, which sends the girls into fits of giggles.

It's a lighthearted moment that only children can provide. I roll my eyes and try to chuckle along with them, but I'm distracted by the way Tony thoroughly rubs the sanitizer into each nail bed, and between his fingers, and up his arms.

What is down there? I wonder.

Once his hands are clean, Tony reaches for his phone in the glove box. He presses a few buttons. He checks his watch. Then, looking a little panicked, he digs in my duffle bag for my phone.

A gust of wind tugs at my beach towel as I stare at Tony's back for a long moment. "Tony?"

Tony's by my side in an instant, putting a hand to my forehead, rubbing my arm gently with his sticky, sanitized palm. "We usually have service here. I can't explain it."

"How about the radio?"

Tony looks toward the front of the boat, a glimmer of hope in his eyes, then shakes his head sadly.

"When I picked up the boat this morning, my dad told me that mice ate through some wire in the radio system over the winter . . . I didn't think it'd be a big deal."

I sigh. "We're stuck—like, thoroughly stuck—right?"

He nods. "There's a huge, tangled nest of fishing line wrapped around our prop, and ... something else—I think the anchor brought it up. If I had a good set of scissors, it would take me an hour at most."

"Pocketknife?"

He chuckles sadly. "Remember when I brought my nephews out here fishing last fall? One of them dropped it into the water. I forgot to buy a replacement knife for the glove box. It's down there," he looks over the edge, "along with the miles of fishing line that ensnared our propeller."

I swallow the heavy lump that's building in my throat and look around. There's nobody on the causeway. Not one jogger or mountain biker we could signal for help. It's never crowded at Porcupine, but the banks are unusually still, apart from the willows and aspens billowing in the growing breeze. "No knife. No radio. And no phone?"

Tony lowers his head and his hands begin to shake.

He's starting to unravel, and I'm wracking my brain for ideas. I used to work in cellular phone sales, there has to be some way to get signal strength— "What if we turn the phones to roaming? Maybe we can pick up another carrier's signal?"

Tony's eyes light up as he reaches for his phone, adjusts the settings, and waits. "C'mon, c'mon . . ." He sighs a shaky breath and reaches for my phone. "Oh, come—*on!*"

"What about analog signal?" My voice sounds too hopeful, I don't know what the newest smartphones are capable of. "Old cell phones used to offer both analog and digital ..."

But that was a decade ago. These days, we run on digital, high-tech confidence.

I watch Tony thumb through the features on his touch screen as the wind picks up.

I close my eyes and lower my head before Tony even says the words.

"There isn't an analog option on our phones now. And I'm

not leaving you alone. Maybe we could swim to shore and walk back to the car? Do you think you could swim from here? Or back float? I could pull you."

A roll of thunder rumbles up the canyon.

I squint into the wind. Black clouds are moving in. They're headed our way.

We're as far as we can get from the boat dock. The closest land is the sheer rock cliff beside us, where I saw something shining earlier. We're all in life vests, but I don't know if I can move in open water at this point. And the wind is making the water choppy.

"Not in my condition. Not to mention the girls, and the fact that we'd be swimming against the wind. Um," I feel the early tensing sensation of another contraction and bite my lip.

Tony sees me bracing for the next one. With three previous deliveries under our belts, he knows the warning signs of a contraction. With pity in his eyes, he sighs, "I'm sorry, of course you can't swim. That was a dumb idea." Gently, he sits beside me and puts an arm around my shoulders.

I inhale—and throw my eyes open.

The smell of rotting, festering lake on his skin is nauseating.

I race to the back and hurl over the edge of the boat.

My hands grip the ladder that Tony just climbed as my body convulses over and over, the latest contraction amplifying my urge. My knuckles are tight by the time I can finally breathe again, but that smell is still there, carried on the breeze from the water below.

I wipe my mouth on the shoulder of my sundress and gaze into the water. As the episode fades, I begin to look at this moment abstractly. It's amazing how fast things disappear in the dark water. Carried by the currents and the gravity and the wind-driven waves, my vomit floats away and dissolves into tiny molecules. I don't think I'll ever be able to swim here again.

I don't realize I'm moaning until Tony tries to guide me back to the bench to lay down.

"June?" he calls, wrapping his arms around me, trying to lift me.

"No," I manage to say through my moans. "Not yet. I can't move yet."

When I finally stop seeing stars and try to stand up, I feel a fresh trickle of warm moisture slide down my inner thighs.

"Tony!" I call out.

"I'm right here," he murmurs.

Thunder rumbles down the canyon.

I groan. "My water just broke." Things couldn't get any worse. And I'm about to have a baby.

I crumple into him.

"Kids!" he calls. They're playing up by the captain's seat. "One, two, three!"

"And on the seat!" A gust of wind drowns out their voices. They race to the bench, concern in their expressions.

"We're going to play a little game." Tony gently sets me in the captain's chair and opens the glovebox.

Tony has them play is a finding game. He wants them to search every cubby and crevice of the boat for something sharp, like scissors, or a knife. "It needs to be sharp enough to cut some fishing line. But don't touch it if you find it," he says. "I don't want you to cut yourself. Just tell me if you see something sharp. The person who finds it wins a new toy, whatever you want."

Little Avery points at the edge of the metal that supports the window. "Is this sharp?"

Tony pulls the contents from the glove box, the lock box, and the hatch that leads to the motor. He finds a compass, a lighter, a few maps, fishing licenses, and a dock fee stub, but not much else.

Then it starts to rain.

Tony Galleo

We're huddled on the floor of the boat, rocking to and fro in the wind and pounding rain. The kids are nestled on either side of June's legs, shielding her lower half and themselves with one of the big beach towels. They almost look like they could be playing London Bridge.

There's a metallic taste in the air. I jump at a clap of thunder. It's so loud, like a firework in a tin can. Little Avery starts to cry.

"Carmella? Gia? Can you girls hug Avery and try to stay warm?"

I'm behind June's head, holding another towel over her. She's wearing her wrinkled hat for added shelter and I can't see her expression. Waves hit the hull in crashing thuds, the storm pelts us with rain, and lightning crackles overhead. The floor of the boat is filling with frigid rainwater. An inch at first, then another.

"Is the boat going to sink?" Carmella asks.

"No way. We just have to wait for the rain to stop and then we'll splash around in it, okay?"

June is trying to breathe as another contraction begins. "We need to get to shore," June moans.

Since her water broke, the contractions have started to mean business. I check the time on my smart watch. Still about five minutes apart, maybe four. And no signal.

I pull the towel taut over June's head. "It'll be over soon."

Our boat is rocking side to side in the wind—will it make June sick again? The water sloshing around in the boat is unnerving. "It'll be over soon," I repeat.

"How do you know? It could last all night!" June's lip is quivering.

She thinks I'm lying to comfort her, but it can't last more than an hour, can it?

My words should give her hope, but she's humming with each breath now.

I'm shaking and my teeth begin to chatter, so I breathe hard to try to warm myself as my exposed back is pelted with rain. We have one more towel, but I won't use it after cleaning my hands with it.

It's going in the trash. Or in an evidence bag.

I shudder again, this time from the conjured memory.

Soon? I said soon? If I don't believe it anymore, how can June?

I'm making an alternate plan, one that involves using one of the bench cushions as a flotation device for June, when something shifts in the air. As the rain drops begin a diminuendo, growing slower and quieter as the winds die down, I sigh with gratitude.

Even though it feels like an hour huddled under our towels, it's only been about twenty minutes so far, and as this contraction passes the rain starts to let up.

Then I hear a rustling. The sound is coming from behind me, from the ladder.

"Help!"

A voice, if it is a voice, hangs in the air like dry powder.

I look around at my family, but nobody seems to hear it, only me. More rustling sounds waft through the breeze. My imagination runs wild—images of peeling white skin trapped inside the web of fishing line. Then, lighter than a whisper, I hear the faint sound again.

"Help!"

June is quiet at the moment. The voice isn't hers.

And it isn't coming from me.

I'm completely unable to form words right now. My jaw is now clenched from the cold dread running through me.

When I think that I can safely take a peek, I turn and do a double take as a muddy arm reaches out for me.

"Oh!" I fall back, flailing, splashing in the water at the bottom of the boat.

June gasps as I bolt to a standing position, my arms suspended midair, ready to fight. I catch my balance and come face to face with a blue-lipped and sickly pale face, and I struggle to breathe. It's the dead man. The dead man in the water.

Then I notice that it's only a boy, around ten years old. He's dressed the same as the dead man. His blue Scout shirt is disheveled, missing a button, and the troop numbers are peeling from the sleeve. Troop 413. His dripping blond hair is matted at odd angles. His feet are barefoot, and his jeans are slimy brown.

"Help me," he mouths.

If it's possible for a voice to sound like dust, like rubbing a worn chalkboard eraser across cracked knuckles, his voice does.

Because it contrasts starkly with his dripping wet frame, the dry sound has a haunting quality.

Suddenly I realize that the boy, sopping wet, is climbing aboard.

I look around to the shoreline, searching for someone that might have pulled up during the storm, but I can't see anybody else. We are the only ones on the water, our truck is the only vehicle on the dirt road beside the dock. "Where did you come from?"

"The water."

I have no reason to doubt him. His lips are swollen and blue. "Are you cold?"

He nods. "Sort of."

I hand him the towel from the corner of the boat and he wraps it around his shoulders stiffly. I need to find out more about him. "How long have you been here?"

He whispers, "Two days, I think."

My eyes widen. "What happened? Did you get separated from your Scout troop?"

He shakes his head. "We were canoeing," he whispers. "I think we drowned."

I gulp. "Who? Your Scout troop?"

"No, my dad and me."

"What's your name?"

"Ryan Wahlbourn." His voice is solemn, making his introduction sound more like an epitaph. Cold. Concrete. Final. "Can you help me and my dad?"

"Where is your dad?"

"He's in the water. We're stuck."

"Where?" I look around the reservoir, but I don't see anybody. An uneasy feeling settles into my gut. His skin is flaking in big white patches. "Ryan, we're stuck, too. But I promise I'll help you if I can."

He shivers again.

I sigh. "You're cold. I wish I could build a fire."

The boy reaches into his fanny pack and retrieves flint and steel with an apologetic look.

"Yeah, I struggled with that when I was in Scouts, too. I've got a lighter, but I can't light a fire in the boat ... Wait a minute! You have a Scout Kit! Do you have a pocketknife?"

"Yeah," the boy says, pulling it out of his fanny pack. It's a shiny new red Swiss army knife.

"Ah, this is great!" I gasp. "This is very helpful. Can I borrow it?"

Ryan clutches his knife to his chest. "Do you swear to give it back to me? It was a birthday gift."

"I swear. Ryan, this knife will help me cut the line that's entangled in my motor so I can take my wife to the hospital. I swear I'll give it back. And I can help get you home."

"My dad, too?"

"Yes, I'll help your dad, too. Where are you from?"

"Brigham--"

"Brigham City? We're from Perry."

June starts breathing heavily again.

"She's having a boy," Ryan says.

I blink. "Actually, the ultrasound says it's a girl."

"It's a boy." Ryan glowers.

"Okay, okay! I guess we'll see. If I can cut the fishing line away from the motor, we might be able to get us to the hospital in time. Ryan, I need your knife to cut the line. Please?"

I stretch my hand out to him.

Ryan swallows hard, then gives the knife to me.

Beneath the soaked beach towels, I can hear June crying. "June?" I pull the towel away. She's worse. Pale and shaking, she's cuddling with the girls.

June gasps when she sees the boy beside me, and the girls' expressions turn from cold misery to shock.

"June? Girls? This is Ryan. He's a lost Boy Scout. He's loaning me his pocketknife. I'm going to cut us free while the girls give him something to eat. Carmella, grab a popsicle. Gia, get a granola bar?" The girls are stiff as they slowly move to help Ryan.

I tie the knife to Ryan's flint and steel cord, then tie that cord around my wrist; if I were to lose this knife, we would all be done for.

Back in the water, I dive under the boat, and come face to face with the old familiar horror. Earlier, I hadn't seen a face yet. Just a hand.

The face is worse.

But not that different from Ryan's. The swollen eyes. The bruised cheeks. The Webelos neckerchief floating around his face.

He bobs in the same water that I do. The current touching him, is touching me.

I surface, gagging and sputtering. I can't do this.

I hear June up on deck, another contraction. If I can't do this, what will happen to her?

I can't do this, but I must. So I do.

With each huge gulp of air, I dive under the boat, push the floating corpse aside, and cut us free of the line. When the bulk is cleared, I find a huge knot still wrapped around the propeller.

I swim to the surface for more air, and the corpse follows. Panic builds in my chest as he floats freely. Peeling patches. Troop 413. This must be Ryan's father. Does Ryan know he's dead?

I cringe as the corpse bobs to the surface, face down. Even if it is Ryan's father, I can't bring him aboard—the kids can't see this. It's good that the children are distracted helping Ryan. They haven't noticed the corpse in the water yet.

With these thoughts swirling within me, I have no choice but to dive again.

Underwater, I see that the tangle is almost clear.

I slice at the line and pull more strands free, and I begin to really wonder about Ryan. Where did he come from? How did he make it to our boat? When he said "we drowned" did he mean to include himself? How is he alive? Or, is he alive?

My lungs are getting used to filling with air and holding it in till they burn. I'm able to cut the last line away this time, and the motor is free. I climb aboard.

"We're free. Let's go."

I'm breathless, sopping wet, and exhausted. I don't realize how still everyone else is, until the twins cry, "Daddy?"

I'm about to start the motor, but the sound of their voices stops me in my tracks.

"What—" I turn. June is on the wet floor, holding the boy, her sundress soiled and muddy from his dirty clothes. She's gently touching the boy's matted hair. "He just fell over," June began, then started to cry. "I don't think he's doing very well."

I kneel beside them. "Ryan? Are you hurt?"

He shakes his head. "I need to get back in the water. I need to go back to my dad. I helped you, and now I need you to help me and my dad. Come back for us? Please?"

A moment of understanding passes between us. "I understand, Ryan. I promise I'll come back."

"What do you mean?" June asks.

I rest my hand on June's shoulder. I won't tell her about the body in the water.

"I know this is hard, but trust me. We need to listen to him. Remember, he saved us today." I turn to Ryan. "We're leaving, but I promise I'll come back."

Ryan nods. I don't know if he's going to crawl back down the ladder to rejoin his father, or if he's going to stay, but I need to help June get to shore. "I'm gonna see if the boat will start." I pat June on the shoulder and step to the captain's chair to turn the key. It starts. The loud rumble comforts me as I raise the anchor and hit the throttle.

We're flying across the water toward the little dirt boat dock where our SUV is parked.

This whole ordeal is coming to a swift and happy close, until I hear, "I need to stay with my dad!" Ryan's voice is raised, he sounds urgent.

"No!" I hear June shout.

I turn just in time to see Ryan climb onto the bench and jump over the edge. I slow the boat. With teary eyes, the girls look from June, to me, and back to the ledge where Ryan jumped. There's no sign of him in our wake. Like a shadow, he dissolved into the water and disappeared.

"Ryan!" I turn the boat around to look for him.

Is Ryan really dead, too? But . . . his lips were so blue. His skin so pale.

We call his name, even June calls from her position on the floor of the boat, but there is no response. We circle the lake. The surface is smooth. Nothing is floating on it, no nest of fishing line, no corpse, and no Ryan.

The girls are perched on the bench, searching the lake. But we can't see boy whose dirty Scout uniform stained June's dress, who also loaned me his pocketknife to free us from our predicament. His pocketknife still dangles from my wrist. I promised I'd give it back. "Ryan!"

June cries out as another contraction begins. "We're going to have the baby on this boat if we don't hurry!" She wears a helpless expression as the contraction takes hold.

"I think," I begin to voice my suspicions. "I don't know how, but think he's been out here for a while." I nod meaningfully, and I feel a tear slip down my cheek.

She nods, too. "I think you're right. We'll come back for him. Okay?" She grits her teeth as another wave hits. "We'll come back and keep your promise."

June's water broke over an hour ago. I look across the water and grip Ryan's pocketknife. "I swear, Ryan. I'll come back for you."

The next morning, after June gives birth to a small but healthy five-pound baby *boy*, I keep that promise.

I'm under a pop-up tent beside a stack of water bottles, a first aid kit, and a table where a topographical map has been laid out. There is a big X on the map, drawn there because that's where I pointed. A white board beside the map shares gathered intel:

Ryan W.

Webelos troop 413.

The police find a vehicle upriver. License plate 555 BCW. A voice comes through the radio. The vehicle owner's wife has been notified. She told the police that her husband and son were on a weeklong trip to test their gear for an upcoming Scout camp out.

I nod sadly as someone writes two names on the whiteboard. Steven Wahlbourn, 34, and Ryan Wahlbourn, age 11.

Because Ryan and his father weren't due home until tomorrow, they weren't even reported as missing yet.

Someone has satellite Wi-Fi on a sturdy laptop. I watch them pull up Doppler Radar history to study the weather events for the past week. A storm came through the area on the first day, and a call to utility maintenance confirms that a lightning strike took out the cell tower. This is added to the white board. I have a hunch that their canoe capsized in the storm.

It doesn't take long for the whistles to sound. The radio nearby starts buzzing again.

The dive team has found the canoe.

I feel restless. I already know what they'll find. And who they'll find.

It's just a matter of time.

I sigh and walk down to the beach. Search and rescue, the local sheriff's department, and the forest service are all at the scene, methodically combing the reservoir in boats and flying drones across the water. The dive team is positioned near the cliffs where June first lost her hat. Where the anchor brought Ryan's father up.

A question surfaces. June saw something shiny when her hat fell into the water. What was it? Timing was everything that afternoon, starting with June pointing at the shiny thing and losing her hat as a result. I need to know what caught her eye but search and rescue doesn't want me out on the water.

I plead my case with the first in command. "I swore to come back for him. I have to know."

After a long pause, he nods. I'm fitted with a life vest, and I climb onto a jet ski behind him. We maneuver across the reservoir that is crowded with search and rescue, careful to leave plenty of space between us and the dive team as we skirt along the water's edge. Search parties are combing the woods on either side of the cliff.

"Ryan!" they call.

How do I tell them they won't find him on the shore?

"Ryan?" I echo. Along the cliff wall, a small bush grows out over the water's edge, and on one of the limbs, something shiny catches my eye. We draw closer and I see a brand-new Scout mirror, tied to a silver fishing lure. It glistens in the midday sun.

I reach for it and pull it off the limb. On the back, in child's handwriting, is a name.

Ryan.

The shiny thing.

Suddenly it's clear. Stuck against the cliff after they capsized, Ryan was signaling for help.

"Ryan," I whisper. "I'll give your pocketknife to your mom, so she can give it back to you."

I don't know how, but Ryan must hear me.

"Over here!" someone calls on the bank nearby, pointing toward the water. "There's a boy ... in the moss!"

The diving team sounds their whistle. The radio chatter is clear. Both Ryan and his dad have been found.

Gripping Ryan's shiny mirror in my hand, I whisper reverently. "Ryan, thank you. Thank you for helping us."

At the funeral, I give Ryan's mother the pocketknife that saved us. She lovingly places it in her son's helpful hands before the casket closes.

As for the mirror, I hang the shiny thing over our infant son's crib, where it twirls at the center of his mobile while he sleeps, and one day I will tell him of the boy who climbed onto our boat and saved us all.

14

AUGUST
ALICE M. BATZEL

I turn the calendar page and pause.
Today, August begins.
Scarce is cool summer shade.
Sweltering dry heat lingers.

Farmers' fields and home gardens are in harvest.
Kitchen counters creek and groan
with heavy ripened fruits and vegetables
awaiting hot water baths and pressure canners.

Distant summer fires spill over mountains.
The evening sun turns red.
Smoke billows skyward.
The horizon is a purple haze.

Absent is the laughter of children
running through sprinklers in the summer yard.
A dear old friend's funeral this past week.
His granddaughter holds a new babe in her arms.

I water my small garden with a mask on my face.
Smoke creeps in silence and chokes me.
Little birds briefly chirp and dance at my feet,
but soon take flight.

Nature's flames burn closer,
displacing many each day.
I awakened to flames invading the valleys.
A nearby farm is lost to the blaze.

15

A VOICE IN THE THUNDER

MCKEL JENSEN

"Mom!" Charlie appeared at his mom's side of the bed, clinging to the blanket. His pajamas were wet and his mom could only see his shadow.

Startled, his mom sat up quickly, and pulled the tassel of her bedside lamp. A storm had rolled in overnight. She had heard the thunder, pulled her boy closer, and kissed his head. "It was just thunder, Sweetheart. There is nothing to worry about," she said.

Urine stuck to his pajamas, saturating the room with its smell. "Let's get you cleaned up," she said and began to escort her son back to his room.

"Mom!" Charlie exclaimed not as loudly, but just as urgent. Charlie's frustration peaked higher as he followed his mom down the hallway and into his room where she started shifting through his drawers looking for a clean pair of pants and some clean undies.

The doorway framed Charlie's silhouette as he stood there, watching his mom slowly blinking her eyes open. He was shaking all over, sweating even. A siren started in the distance outside.

"Mom," he said again, but just louder than a whisper, "I'm not afraid of thunder." His breathing steadied, and his face grew serious. "It was the voice inside it."

Brigham City was nestled against the wayward side of the Wasatch Mountain Range. When storms rolled through, the wind blew from west to east. Violent storms somehow traveled the opposite direction. Every time a storm threatened the city, a siren whined. Not the sound of a nuclear attack or a tornado warning, but a subtle, background sound that was easy to dismiss. The whining had become so commonplace that no one noticed it much. The only time the sound was brought to the forefront was when a newcomer asked about the significance of the sound, or when a child heard it and asked. Most people believed that the siren warned of lightning for the railway workers or for a local company with a lot of electrical equipment. If you asked Otis Warren, the oldest resident in Brigham City, he would have said that what you were actually hearing was an echo; not an actual echo like reverberations off the mountain, but an echo from a past that no one seemed to remember—a past that should stay in the past.

Everyone knew Otis lived in one of the two-story 100-year-old farm houses that dotted the streets of the small city. When his father bought it, the house stood alone on the block. But with each passing decade, his father parceled the land and new houses filled the space. When his parents died, Otis put the title under his name and began to maintain the property. As the years passed, and after two knee replacements and one heart surgery, the neighborhood saw that maintaining a large home was not as easy as it had been. Otis let go of fixing the chipped plaster, let the gate's squeak remain, and mainly moved to first floor living.

Otis often sat on his porch swing that overlooked his lawn and the street in front of his house.

Charlie often saw him when he rode passed on his way home from school. Charlie didn't know Otis, but he knew of him. Otis and his house was a fixture, something that was just always there, even if not officially acquainted.

Charlie always thought Otis was just as big, old, and as run down as that old house. Once, when Charlie rode his bike passed, he swore that he saw Otis laughing out loud to no one, which only made Charlie peddle faster. "That man must be crazy," he said to himself, unclear if it was Otis or the house that made him uneasy. Even when Otis wasn't out on his porch swing, Charlie felt eyes on him as he passed.

The day after the thunderstorm, while Charlie was riding home from school, his bike jolted to a stop right in front of Otis' house, and he crashed.

"Argh!" Charlie yelled. When he lifted up his bike, he noticed a stick in the spokes and the frame of the wheel was bent. Charlie cleared the few pebbles that had been encased in his knee and tried to clear the knot in his throat. But as much as he tried, it just kept getting tighter.

As he attempted to get his backpack off the ground, he froze. Someone was standing behind him. He heard boots scuffling on the pavement. He wanted to look, but his body wouldn't follow. He felt stuck, afraid to turn around.

"Need help, boy," Otis' scruffy, low voice bellowed.

"I'm a…" Charlie stammered. "I'm a…." Charlie didn't know what to do. Should he run? If so, should he leave his bike?

"Are you hurt, boy?" Otis said.

"I'm…" Charlie said. "No."

"Well then, get up," Otis commanded.

Charlie stood and the two looked at each other awkwardly. Charlie noticed Otis' thick boots, baggy high-waisted jeans, and a worn-out button-down shirt. Underneath Otis' gray frock of hair and white eyebrows, he was clean-shaven.

Charlie caught the man observing him.

Otis bent down to inspect the bike. "Are you the Wilson boy?"

"Yes." Charlie answered, clearly not wanting to keep this dialogue going.

"There is something different about you, isn't there?" Otis asked.

Charlie reached up to his smaller ear—a deformity he's had since birth, but it didn't feel like Otis was referring to his ear. It took a moment for Charlie to answer. "I guess," he puttered, not taking his eyes off of Otis but wanting to.

"You'll need a new rim," Otis said and stepped away from the bike.

Charlie barely whispered a "thank you" before hesitantly starting home, pushing his bike with the handlebars as it wobbled.

Before Charlie reached the corner, he heard Otis say aloud to no one, "Yeah, you're right. There is something different about that boy," before heading up the path to his porch.

By the time Charlie reached home, his interest in that two-story house and the old man had grown. He didn't know how Otis knew his name. *Of course something is different with me,* he thought, but he knew that his ear wasn't the only thing that made him unique. *He doesn't even know me.* Charlie grew more defensive. There is no possible way that the old man would know about the voices he hears during the thunderstorms. The ear was easy to explain; voices in thunder, however, was a whole different level of strange that he certainly didn't want to attach to himself.

A few days later, a cool rain swept through the small city and the clouds threatened a darker storm. Charlie had nothing holding him back anymore. He ran through the rain and paused in the front of Otis' house. Panting, Charlie ran up the path, stepped right past the swaying porch swing and proceeded to knock.

The floorboards shifted as the old man came to the door.

"What's going on, boy? What can I do for you?"

Charlie didn't know if these were questions or demands.

"Why did you call me different?" he blurted out.

Otis looked at the boy.

"Tell me," Charlie continued, rain dripping off of him.

"Have a seat," Otis said.

It may have been the loose floorboards or the incoming wind, but Charlie swore the porch swing swayed more when they approached it, as if someone was getting off.

Haunted or not, all fear had left Charlie. He wanted answers and wouldn't leave until he got them.

Otis braced his knee with his hands before sitting down on the step, wincing a little. He then looked sternly into Charlie's eye and asked, "Do you hear them?"

"Hear what? Who?" Charlie was now feeling defensive. *How does he know?* Only his mom knew about the voices.

"You know what I'm talking about," Otis said directly. "When the sirens sound. When there is thunder."

He *did* know.

Otis asked again, "What do you hear?"

"Voices," Charlie muttered, spittle flinging from his mouth. "Voices. Screams."

"Do you know the types of voices?" Otis asked calmly. "Are

they men, children, women…" he spoke as if there were more to choose from.

"Men. Grown men. Loud, like they are in pain. They, they scream like they are being tortured." Charlie winced at the word *torture* but was relieved to be able to share his secret. He felt no judgement from Otis, but was still hesitant to trust.

Otis took a breath and nodded his head slightly. "Charlie," he started, "do you know about the prison that was here several years ago—long before you were born, and definitely long before your family moved to this north end of town?"

"No," said Charlie, "Brigham City never had a prison."

"Oh, yes it did," Otis interrupted. "It did and no one likes to talk about it, and when no one talks about things, they think they disappear. I bet you think those voices will disappear if you don't talk about them. But have they? Have they disappeared?"

Charlie's mouth opened, but he wasn't sure how to answer.

"My daddy," Otis continued, "worked at the prison. It was called the Wasatch Men's Penitentiary. He actually enjoyed some of the inmates and when those inmates were released, he would continue the friendship outside those walls. I remember one or two ex-convicts had no place to go after they were released, so he would have them stay with us." Otis smiled, obviously thinking of the kindness his father rendered.

"Your dad let convicts live in your house?" Charlie asked.

"*Ex*-convicts," he corrected. "Some weren't so bad. Many were in for mild offences, though you are right—many had done some pretty nasty things, and my dad made sure they didn't get close to us. He also knew that many people couldn't survive on their own after getting out. The world changes quickly when you aren't there to observe it. It doesn't matter if they served one year or twenty, the world is a different place when they are released."

"What about the voices? What does a prison have to do with the voices I hear?" Charlie asked.

"Now wait a minute. I don't want to give an impression that the place was sunshine and green grass behind those barbed wire fences. My daddy tried to bring a little bit of kindness into those halls. But in spite of his efforts, he could always feel the darkness there. Then he witnessed something that could have cost him his life."

Charlie's breath caught before Otis insisted that he drink some water.

"There, boy," Otis said. "Sit back and I'll tell you about it."

As the boy settled into his chair—a chair that was older than his mother, he kept his eyes keenly on the old man.

"Well," Charlie said trying to be patient and failing, "What was it? What did your dad witness?"

Otis leaned forward, his voice became deep and steady. "The answer to that question lies sixty years in the past."

Lightning cut through the dark over the concrete structure of Wasatch Men's Penitentiary. A siren wailed, almost deafening to the inmates inside. Seconds later, booming thunder threatened to crack their cell floors as if Hell itself were opening up beneath them. Putrid smells of sweat, mold, and whatever had stewed for dinner permeated the 5- by 9-foot cells as darkness settled around the occupants of each bed.

Another flash of light and the deep bellow of thunder reverberated in Pete's soul. The siren barely covered the screams of the other inmate. "That was Chester Holt," Pete said to himself. Then he counted, "Next will be Sydnie Rockerson, Benny Li, Big T, then," he paused. He wanted to vomit, but the thought of tasting that dinner again made him push it back down.

"Rockerson!" A guard yelled. Two guards tackled a man in a jumpsuit. Two small men in lab coats stood in the background making notes and trying to stay out of the way. Rockerson, with the help of the guards, followed the men in lab coats through the heavy doors at the end of the hall.

"Pete," the man by the name of Big T yelled out. "Pete!"

"Yeah, Big T," Pete answered.

"We gotta get outta here. The storm, the noise—" just then another thunder boomed causing them to hold onto the wall for stability. Big T closed his eyes, as if doing so would stop him from hearing the screams. He cussed.

The guards arrived again, taking Benny Li.

"Pete!" Big T said. "Think of something!"

Pete was just as stuck. He felt his number getting closer as well as the void from the cells on his block—even though Rockerson was now back in his cell.

"What if," he couldn't get the words out—any words out. He heard a clink. Sirens started wailing again and footsteps, perhaps the same ten that took Benny Li moments earlier. They brought Benny Li back, but moved to the next cell.

"Thomas Barber," one guard said to the head man in a lab coat. He didn't look smart enough to be wearing a lab coat, but what did Pete know.

"Why," exclaimed the man, "this man is much too big. I don't think it will work."

"What do you mean he won't work," said the man in the other lab coat. "We were supposed to try everyone."

"I'm telling you it won't work," he said with annoyance.

"Fine," the guard said as if he had something better to do.

"Peter Littleton," the guard stated.

The man checked his clipboard and looked at Pete's face. "What did he do?"

"Does it matter?" the guard said.

"No, no. I suppose not." He made a checkmark next to Pete's name on the chart. "Let's bring him. Hurry along, this storm may not last much longer."

Pete heard every sound in the seconds that followed. Every press of a step, the sound of the key hitting the metal door as it nicked the keyhole before it entered, the sigh from Big T next door, the sound the man in the lab coat made as he scratched the collar of his neck before turning the page of his notes, the heart beat in his own chest—but he didn't hear the sirens, the thunder, or his own scream.

"Stop, stop, stop," another man in a lab coat showed up. "This procedure obviously hasn't been working. I've got approval from a higher up to try this one." He held up a vial with contents that seemed to be boiling yet felt cold when it entered Pete's bloodstream. It hurt. It made his muscles tight. It made him sweat and shiver. Pete saw the flash of lightning then braced himself for the inevitable. One-one thousand, two-one thousand, three—. Sirens blared and then he remembered nothing.

When he woke up, the silence of his own mind and his own body surprised him. No thunder. No sirens. All was calm. The darkness had lifted as much as it physically could for a room with no windows.

"Good morning," said a familiar voice. It was friendly and such a contrast from the nightmare he just lived.

"Warren Hal?" Pete asked, blinking his eyes as if blinded, though his room was no brighter than a closet.

"Hey there, Pete," he said. "Seemed like a pretty bad storm last night?"

The look on Hal's face suggested genuine concern. "And what's with this unearthly quite that's here this morning? Usually, you guys get all excited for the change of guard." Hal looked at Pete and didn't move his gaze from Pete's face.

For Pete's entire life he had felt like no one could see him, if fact, that was what inevitably got him in prison—he had to do something big to be noticed. But Warren Hal saw him. It felt good to be seen.

"This is a dark place," Pete stated. "And when there are storms, it's even darker."

"Ay," Warren Hal said. "That storm was pretty big. I heard the storm trigger the sirens."

"The storm doesn't trigger the sirens," Pete interrupted, "we do."

Charlie was both fascinated and repulsed. "What were they doing to them?"

"I'm not really sure," Otis said. "All I know is that nothing good ever went on at the prison during stormy nights."

"What happened to Pete? Who was Warren Hal?" Charlie demanded before taking a breath to stay calm.

"Warren Hal was my father," Otis said. "This was his house. When Pete told him what was going on during the storms, my father did what he could to fix it. It didn't happen until a few weeks after he learned about the truth, but Pete and my father made a plan."

In the prison, Pete opened his napkin at breakfast to read the note Warren Hal left him. *Tomorrow morning*, it said.

This brought a mixture of hope and fear. What could go wrong? The plan was that on his morning checks, right as his shift started, Warren Hal would unlock Pete's cell. That would give Pete plenty of time to get to the supply closet and go through the window before he was discovered. If he was able to make it out, he still had to survive while on the run. If he got caught, he was not only risking a more severe sentence, but Warren Hal would also be persecuted, losing his career, his family, and his life as a free man. The sacrifice was not lost on

Pete. But, as opportunity knocks, opposition takes hold and the night before the escape, another large storm rolled in. For some reason, unlike the other times, the guards and the men in lab coats who claimed to be doctors took him first. Pete was like the chosen one to them now, and the experiment continued as before: bubbling vial, shivers and heat, flash of light, sirens, thunder, and screams. The first time it was performed, Pete felt fuzzy for days after. He never recovered from a feeling of being slightly…*off*, like he was living behind a veil. And he woke up early the next morning in a panic wondering if he had slept too late. He felt even more intangible.

"My daddy said he went in that morning and saw the shape of him under his blankets sleeping calmly," Otis described, "but he never saw his face. He said it wasn't much longer that an alarm sounded and the prison was entirely locked down. Before anyone could fully understand what had happened, my father realized that Pete had made himself disappear. He escaped like a ghost in the night and no one ever knew where he went."

"What do you think happened to him?" Charlie asked.

"I don't think anything," Otis said sternly. "I *know* what happened to him."

Charlie looked confused.

"When Pete made it out," he started, "he didn't feel great. Whatever they gave him made him feel funny. But it wasn't long before he made it out of that prison. My daddy never said how he really did it, but all they ever found of him were his clothes. How a naked escaped prisoner made his way into Brigham City without a single soul seeing him, is a mystery."

Pete worked his way across the field steady, quickly, and quietly. He knew he had a limited amount of time before the alarms would sound. He was tired, and although he had escaped the compound, his body still felt trapped somehow. At one point, he curled up in a field to rest, which he didn't find rational. He couldn't see very well and each time he looked at his hands and body, they seemed different—he almost couldn't see himself. *What did those people give me?* His brain was getting fuzzy and the exertion of running along in a drugged haze made him collapse on the ground. He cut his knee on a rock.

Moments later he woke to the sound of dogs searching the field. They were too close. If he got up and ran, they would surely see him. If he sat—well, he would just be waiting to be found. Without knowing, a dog was already two feet away from him, sniffing the ground where his knee bled. But the dog didn't see him or smell him. He was right in front of them—Pete could see the dog's teeth and smell the guard's aftershave, yet neither the guard nor the dog noticed him. The guard blew a whistle and a group of guards surrounded the small patch of blood. Pete sat there, feet away, stiff, deafened by the sound of his heart drumming in his ears as the scene before him played out in slow motion.

"We found this," said the guard to another. "It still looks pretty fresh. He can't be far from here."

"Great work," the other guard said. "Let's keep going in this direction. We'll have him soon."

Can they be serious? Pete thought. *This can't be real. I'm right here. Do they not see me?*

Pete considered standing and waving his hands in the air, but he thought that would be silly. That would be the exact thing not to do when escaping prison. But there he was, sitting in a field surrounded by dogs and guards hunting for him and they were oblivious.

Warren Hal joined the group's investigation and stared right in Pete's direction. "Hey, fellas," he hollered.

Pete began to panic. Had his friend betrayed him?

"I wonder if he is headed down near the creek," Warren Hal suggested. "If he is wounded, he wouldn't want to leave a trail and the creek seems a logical place to hide."

As he watched the guards and dogs move in a different direction, Pete laid back in the grass in relief. There he waited patiently for hours, and he only decided to move once the activity in the field died down. He was hungry, cold, extremely tired, naked and bleeding somewhere.

He had studied a map that Warren Hal created, piece-by-piece on every dining tray napkin. He was looking for Warren's house—a white, two-story home in the middle of the 700 North block.

He made it as quickly and quietly as he could through the back gate and across the side of the house, being careful not to have anyone see him, but as he passed one window, directly at his eye level, he paused. Against his better judgment, he peeked inside and saw a woman baking. His stomach yearned for food.

There was a young man, just younger than him, sitting at the table, facing the window. The young man was reading text books and then making notes on some papers.

"Otis," the woman said, "Do you need to do your studies on the table? We are going to have dinner soon."

As the young man shifted, Pete instinctively stepped back from the window to hide, but something caught his attention that made him linger. As Pete leaned in toward the window, it wasn't the inhabitants of the house that concerned him, but his own reflection. He expected to see a gaunt, slim, hairless face, but he saw nothing. Where his face should be, stood a tree and the hedge behind him. He looked down. He had no body. That medicine the men in lab coats gave him literally made him disappear. He was invisible. He fell to the ground from shock.

Sometime later, he woke up to Warren Hal's familiar voice coming from inside, only he was speaking to his wife.

"I'm just concerned for him," Hal said, as their son continued his studies from the coffee table. "I think something has happened."

"It's been hours since I heard the reports," she said. "I expected him a while ago."

Pete steadied himself, which was its own kind of challenge since he couldn't see his own legs and with no other option, he walked up to the back door and knocked.

"You mean to tell me that your parents harbored an escaped convict?" asked Charlie.

"Yes," Otis replied.

Charlie didn't know where to begin with his questions.

"Perhaps you should focus more on the fact that our government conducted experiments on prisoners," Otis suggested. "Those men may not have been exactly innocent, but they did not deserve that."

"What happened to him?" Charlie asked.

"Pete stayed a while," he said. "We needed to make sure that he was safe and had what he needed before we could send him on his way. Besides, being so close to the prison was scary for us, too. If the authorities had caught my daddy, well," he paused, "well, we wouldn't be sitting here having this conversation on these steps here."

This was a lot for Charlie to take in. "What does this have to do with me? With what I hear?"

"The voices," Otis paused, "are the echoes of those men that no longer wish to remain silent. Perhaps they want to be heard," he looked at Charlie before continuing. "And it looks like they are finding a way."

Charlie stared a moment at a scuff on the floor. "Why the sirens, then?" he asked.

"Back then, the sirens were used to cover the screams of the inmates that the lightning caused," Otis said. "It's a terrible thing, if you ask me. All set up to hide their madness from the community around them."

Charlie got up without asking anything else. He scratched behind his small ear, looked down at his feet and began to walk home, leaving his bike on Otis' lawn.

A week passed and the annual Brigham City Peach Days festival was underway. Charlie and his friends rode as many carnival rides as they had money for and gorged themselves with Pit Burgers and peach milkshakes.

As they moved deeper into the crowd, Charlie noticed the sky change. He heard something past the whirl of the carnival around them—a merciless, whining call.

"Do you guys hear that?" Charlie asked.

His friends looked confused and shook their heads.

"The sirens! Do you hear them?"

As the wind picked up, the sky got darker, and rain began to fall in sheets. The carnival goers ran for cover.

Charlie stood still, facing the storm. Lighting broke up the blackness of the sky as the siren bellowed louder in Charlie's ear.

Crowds watched the storm from the easements of the Willow Glenn Bank building on the side of the street. Thunder rumbled the buildings, but something more primal and unearthly dominated the air—a boy, alone in the street, taunting the storm.

"I hear you!" Charlie shouted at the storm. "I hear your cries."

The wind picked up the back of Charlie's jacket and he had

to bow his head to keep his balance. One instant later, rain blanketed his face.

"I hear you!"

Thunder descended as if simultaneously emitting from both the sky and the ground. People that lined the streets covered their ears. Some began to cry.

"Your voices don't scare me anymore," Charlie bellowed. "You are free. I hear you!"

Another flash of lightning and the rumbling of thunder began to crescendo.

"I hear you!" someone yelled, but it wasn't Charlie's voice but came from someone at his side. It took Charlie by surprise to see Otis joining him out in the street. He made eye contact with him before turning back to the storm.

Thunder came again, and Charlie and Otis stood unwavered.

"I hear you. We know what happened to you," Charlie said just above a whisper. "We hear you," he said again before collapsing to the ground.

When Charlie woke up moments later on the wet pavement, he was unable to see the faces of those surrounding him. Paramedics waved a bright flashlight across his face to check his eyes for dilation. His body relaxed into exhaustion when he realized the wind, rain, and thunder had ended.

Weeks passed and fall was in its full glory in Brigham City. At school, Ms. Rina had given her class an assignment to share a part of Brigham City history. That day, Charlie spoke about the prison that used to be on the north end of town. Of course, some had heard the story after Charlie appeared on the front page of the Box Elder News Journal because of what happened at Peach Days. The highlight of the infamous prison was printed on page three.

"How did your presentation go?" Otis asked Charlie as he walked up the front steps of the old two-story house.

"I think it went good," Charlie said, throwing his printed report on the porch swing. "I left some things out, but I got the point across. I don't think they would believe me about Pete." In the distance, a siren began to wail.

"That's good," Otis said. "Come on inside and help me with this lightbulb. Do you remember what I told you about different types of lights?"

"I remember," Charlie said.

Pausing at the front door, Charlie asked, "Hey Otis? What ever happened to Pete? Where did he end up?"

Otis looked at Charlie through the screen door, then turned and began walking to the kitchen. "Oh, he's still around," he said.

Charlie followed Otis inside and the screen door close behind him. The bench began to swing and, as if wind had blown across the porch, the pages of Charlie's report began to turn.

ABOUT THE AUTHORS

BETTI AVARI lives in the Rocky Mountains of Northern Utah, where nature, friends, and family play crucial roles in her life. Betti fuels her creativity with her curiously curated life, eclectic travels alongside her daughters, and adventurous spirit. Betti's support includes Stephanie Gittins, The Clandestine Writerhood Guild, and her family with their tireless support of her passion. Previous publications include: *Arachnivorous* published 2018, *Roadkill* published 2019, *Tears of a Clown* published 2019, *Limber Lumber* published 2019, *Brigham City Sunshine & Moonshine* 2019, and *Where Gulls Dance* published 2021. Betti says, "Believe in the beauty of your dreams—and nightmares—because life's too short not to."

ALICE M. BATZEL is a published author, playwright, journalist, and poet from the Northwest Florida Gulf Coast. She has published with Pioneer Drama Service, Inc., JAHIMA of Chicago, Box Elder Magazine, Latter-day Saint Publishing and Media Association, The OdieGroup Press, Willow Park Press, The Writers' Cache, and as a guest writer with various newspapers. Alice studied at Utah State University, Northwest Florida State College, and the AHIMA of Chicago. Her current writing projects include poetry, humor, short stories, novels, essays, stage scripts, magazine articles, and a collection of Christmas stories. Alice and her husband enjoy living in a peaceful rural community at the foot of a majestic mountain range in northern Utah. Readers can visit her website www.alicembatzel.com and connect with her on her Facebook author page https://www.facebook.com/people/Author-Alice-M-Batzel/100034795072248

JOSEPH BATZEL holds a master's degree in Theater and Cinematic Arts and a Bachelor's in Speech and Dramatic Arts from Brigham Young University. He has presented workshops in public reading skills and audiobook narration for the League of Utah Writers and the Latter-day Saint Publishing and Media Association. He is also the former director of Education of LDSPMA. He has worked as a professional actor, director, casting director, associate producer, and writer for stage and film. Additionally, he is an independent narrator and producer of audiobooks and hosts his podcast "How Did I Get Here." He presently is an adjunct faculty member for Utah State University, teaching courses in creative arts and public speaking. He resides in northern Utah with his wife Alice; they have two wonderful sons and five beautiful grandchildren. For further information, visit Joseph's website at www.josephbatzel.com

KATHY DAVIDSON lives the dream high up on a hill overlooking beautiful Bear Lake with her talented husband and their large bloodhound, Rufus. She loves watching cloud formations blow across the valley, naming the ones that show up often. After raising three kids, Kathy went back to school and earned a bachelor's degree in English so she felt more confident in following her dream of writing. Her first novel *The House at Dietrich Hollow* is available on Amazon, and she has short stories in three anthologies: *Spirals—A Collection of Poetry & Prose from Utah's Northern Edge*, *Metamorphosis: A Collection of Poetry and Prose*, and *Heard at a UTAH Diner*. Writing in this mixed-up world makes her happy.

MCKEL JENSEN holds a Master of Arts in English from Weber State University where she was selected to be the commencement speaker for her graduating class. She has won awards for her short story "Goblin Creek" and is proud to have her essay "Finding Muchness" published alongside nationally recognized essayists through Full Grown People. Her essay was selected to be part of a larger print anthology called *Soul Mates 101* under the same publisher. Until the birth of her second child, she worked as a technical writer for manufacturing, pharmaceutical and government contracting companies. McKel lives in Brigham City with her husband and three adorable, attention-seeking young children.

Although she wrote her first 4-line poem before entering kindergarten, **DEDE MATTIX** never succumbed to the title of "poet" until taking a writing class taught by Professor Darrell Spencer at BYU in 1984. Since then, despite being sidetracked by the publication of a novel and several short stories, she continues to write and win awards for her poems and is currently at work on a chapbook.

KERI MONTGOMERY is an award-winning short story author in adult speculative fiction. She's a contributing author to *Rise Above Depression*, a #1 Amazon bestseller in self-help by main author and inspirational speaker Jodi Orgill Brown. Keri's short fiction can be found in numerous collections, including the LUW Press anthologies *At First Glance* and *Metamorphosis,* in *Joyride —Tales of First Cars, Classic Cars, and Dreams Cars,* and in *Spirals —A Collection of Poetry & Prose from Utah's Northern Edge. Spirals* went on to receive a 2020 Recommended Read Award from The League of Utah Writers. When not creating fiction, she enjoys museums trips with her kids and wishing for superhuman skills.

MIKE NELSON, a late bloomer in the writing and publication worlds, is an active member of the League of Utah Writers, and holds a Bachelor of Science degree in accounting from Weber State University. Although Mike's primary emphasis in writing is the novel, he has contributed several short-stories to various League and private anthologies. His published novels include: *Thorns of Avarice, Treehouse in the Hood, Clairvoyant* (Awarded The League of Utah Writer's Silver Quill award for adult literature in 2019), *Broken Cowboy, Clairvoyant Book 2,* and *The Highwayman.* In addition, he recently published a collection of short stories, *Mike's Shorts.* He just finished the manuscript for his eighth novel, *Clairvoyant Book 3–The Love Story,* and is currently writing a sequel to *Broken Cowboy.* Writing is one of Mike's passions, and although he has a number of rabid fans, he primarily writes for himself. He says it's the best hobby he's ever had.

VALERIE ODENTHAL loves dabbling in creative projects. She quests to find delightful adventures including: writing creative non-fiction, children's literature, playwriting, storytelling in Box Elder Magazine, and seeking genres that spark her imagination. When not writing, she can be found creating and designing costumes, props, and sets for Heritage Community Theatre, or building interactive exhibits at the Brigham City Museum of Art & History. Her favorite pastimes include teaching crafts or art, road trips, event planning, and seeking the perfect scone. Valerie is joined by her husband, Steve Odenthal, their five children with their families, and more grandkids than will fit under a blanket fort, as they seek all things fun.

E.B. WHEELER is the award-winning author of over a dozen books of history, historical fiction, and historical fantasy, including *Wishwood, The Haunting of Springett Hall,* Whitney Award finalist *Born to Treason,* and *Utah Women: Pioneers, Poets & Politicians,* as well as several short stories, magazine articles, and scripts for educational software programs. She has graduate degrees in history and landscape architecture from Utah State University. The League of Utah Writers named her the Writer of the Year in 2016. Her kidlit work is represented by Abigail Samoun of Red Fox Literary. In addition to writing, she sometimes consults about historic preservation and teaches history.